ACTUAL BIBLICAL PSYCHOLOGY

The Truly Authoritative Approach to Treating People Correctly

Copyright © William J. Luke 2024.
All rights reserved.

To contact the author, email:
bluke.bct@gmail.com

DECLARATION

Actual biblical psychology is based upon **the King James Version [KJV] of the Bible**, because the accuracy and consistency of this version proves that it alone is the true English translation of the Bible.

Contents

Chapter 1
THE FIVE BIBLICAL PRINCIPLES   7

Chapter 2
THE FIVE PARTS TO A PERSON   11

Chapter 3
THE FOUR INFANT RESPONSES   17

Chapter 4
THE THREE ESSENTIAL FACTORS   21

Chapter 5
THE THREE DETRIMENTAL FACTORS   23

Chapter 6
THE FOUR CONSIDERATION METHODS   27

Chapter 7
THE FOUR PERSON TYPES   31

Chapter 8
THE FOUR LOVE LANGUAGES   35

Chapter 9
THE FOUR ATTACHMENT STYLES   39

Chapter 10
THE FOUR RESPONSES TO GOD'S WORD   43

Chapter 11
THE FOUR BELIEFS IN GOD'S WORD   47

Chapter 12
THE FOUR NON-BIASED BEHAVIOUR STYLES   51

Contents

Chapter 13
THE TWO DEGREES OF BIAS   55

Chapter 14
THE SIX BIASED BEHAVIOUR STYLES   61

Chapter 15
THE THREE BIAS PROBLEMS   67

Chapter 16
THE SIX BIAS EFFECTS   71

Chapter 17
THE THREE BIAS SOLUTIONS   77

Chapter 18
THE THREE BIAS TREATMENTS   81

Chapter 19
THE FOUR SPIRITUAL DEVELOPMENT STAGES   85

Chapter 20
THE THREE CHRIST-ATTESTATION LEVELS   89

Chapter 21
THE TWO MEANINGS OF LIFE   93

Chapter 22
THE TWO TREATMENT AIMS   99

Chapter 23
THE TWO PERSON MODELS   101

Chapter 24
THE TWO DEFENSIVE MECHANISMS   105

Chapter 1

THE FIVE BIBLICAL PRINCIPLES

Actual biblical psychology is based on five biblical principles. The five biblical principles are:

The five parts principle
The three elements principle
The three components principle
The four persons principle
The three treatments principle

The Five Parts Principle

The first biblical principle which actual biblical psychology is based upon, is that there are five parts to a person - four living parts and one life-giving part. Mk 12:30; Heb 4:12 [KJV]. The five parts are:

The body [strength] - the experience processing part.
The mind - the knowledge processing part.
The heart - the understanding processing part.
The soul - the information managing part.
The spirit - the life-giving and information carrying part.

The Three Elements Principle

The second biblical principle which actual biblical psychology is based upon, is that there are three elements by which God gives a person the competence to be just, kind and right. Prov 2:6; Col 1:9 [KJV]. The three elements are:

Wisdom - righteous experience in the body.
Knowledge - truthful knowledge in the mind.
Understanding - gracious understanding in the heart.

The Three Components Principle

The third biblical principle which actual biblical psychology is based upon, is that there are three components to the competence that God gives a person. 2 Tim 1:7 [KJV]. The three components are:

Power - righteous feelings in the body.
Love - gracious cares in the heart.
Sound mind - truthful opinions in the mind.

The Four Persons Principle

The fourth biblical principle which actual biblical psychology is based upon, is that there are four person types. Prov 1:5 & 22 [KJV]. The four persons types are:

The wise - the non-biased person type.
The simple - the heart-biased person type.
The scorner - the body-biased person type.
The fool - the mind-biased person type.

The Three Treatments Principle

The fifth biblical principle which actual biblical psychology is based upon, is that there is a treatment for each of the three biased person types. Prov 3:11 & 8:33 & 15:31; 2 Tim 3:16 [KJV]. The three treatments are:

Reproof - of unrighteous experience by righteous experience.
Correction - of untruthful knowledge by truthful knowledge.
Instruction - of gracious understanding by gracious understanding.

Chapter 2

THE FIVE PARTS TO A PERSON

There are five parts to a person - four living parts and one life-giving part. Mk 12:30; Heb 4:12 [KJV]. The five parts to a person are:

The body
The mind
The heart
The soul
The spirit

The Body

The body is the experience processing part of a person. The body [nervous system] has four working areas. The four working areas are:

The experience working area
The feelings working area
The body-lusts working area
The body-memory working area

Experience is practical information gained from external and internal happenings. Experience includes practice, actions, participation, involvement and interactions.

Feelings are sensations formed from experience. Feelings formed from experience of external happenings include sensory feelings. Feelings formed from experience of internal happenings include physiological feelings, emotional feelings and spiritual state feelings.

Sensory feelings include temperature, texture and weight.

Physiological feelings include hunger, fatigue and pain.

Emotional feelings are exclusively joy [happiness, euphoria, ecstasy] and sorrow [sadness, grief, remorse].

Spiritual state feelings include competence, uncertainty, guilt, shame, embarrassment, frustration, stress, anxiety, loneliness, contentment, happiness, hopefulness, boredom, depression, disgust, contempt and anger.

Body-lusts are innate desires of the body. Body-lusts include adultery, lewdness, variance, emulation, wrath, strife, sedition, heresy, envying, drunkenness and revelling.

Body-memory is ingrained information. Body-memory includes muscle memory, automatic responses, and previous sensory, physiological, emotional and spiritual state feelings.

The Mind

The mind is the knowledge processing part of a person. The mind has four working areas. The four working areas are:

The knowledge working area
The opinions working area
The conceits working area
The memories working area

Knowledge is theoretical information acquired from anything. Knowledge includes education, learning, study, recognition and familiarity.

Opinions are judgements formed from knowledge. Opinions include conclusions and preferences.

Conceits are innate inventions of the mind. Conceits include theories, theologies, imaginations, fantasies, vanity and pride.

Memories are stored information. Memories include previous knowledge and opinions.

The Heart

The heart is the understanding processing part of a person. The heart has four working areas. The four working areas are:

The understanding working area
The cares working area
The heart-lusts working area
The emotions working area

Understanding is comprehension of method, meaning, reason and purpose, derived from experience and knowledge. Understanding includes discernment, realization, intuition, empathy, compassion, belief and trust.

Cares are burdens formed from understanding. Cares include loves, wants, intentions, attachments, responsibilities and loyalties.

Heart-lusts are innate desires of the heart. Heart-lusts include gluttony and vile affections such as sodomy.

Emotions are reactions to understanding and cares. Emotions are exclusively joy [happiness, euphoria, ecstasy] and sorrow [sadness, grief, remorse].

The Soul

The soul is the information managing part of a person. The soul has four working areas. The four working areas are:

The conscience working area
The consideration working area
The decision working area
The will working area

Conscience is inherited information. Conscience is exclusively knowledge of what is good [gracious] and what is evil [selfish].

Consideration is deliberation. Consideration includes thinking, examining, pondering and reasoning.

Decision is choice. Decision includes selection, conclusion and resolution.

Will is determination. Will includes attitude and discipline.

The Spirit

The spirit is the life-giving and information carrying part of a person. The spirit is the essence of life, and the information carried in it determines a person's spiritual state.

FOUR LIVING PARTS OF A PERSON

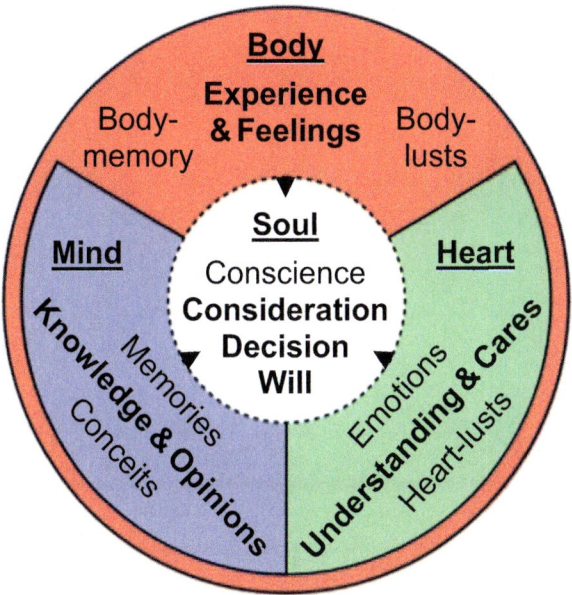

Equal amounts of red, green and blue [RGB] make white. Equal consideration of body, heart and mind make a non-biased soul.

Chapter 3

THE FOUR INFANT RESPONSES

Variable factors, such as the state of an infant's body [nervous system] and the levels of chemicals in them at birth, means that different people are birthed with different responses to stimuli. Mainstream psychology categorizes these differences as four infant responses, termed temperaments. The four infant responses are:

The social infant response
The settled infant response
The slow infant response
The sensitive infant response

The Social Infant Response

Depending on the state of their body [nervous system] and the levels of chemicals in them at birth, a person can be birthed with a social infant response. This means that a person can be birthed with a tendency to be social in response to stimuli. So, for the first few months of their life they are naturally social.

The Settled Infant Response

Depending on the state of their body [nervous system] and the levels of chemicals in them at birth, a person can be birthed with a settled infant response. This means that a person can be birthed with a tendency to be settled in response to stimuli.

So, for the first few months of their life they are naturally settled.

The Slow Infant Response

Depending on the state of their body [nervous system] and the levels of chemicals in them at birth, a person can be birthed with a slow infant response. This means that a person can be birthed with a tendency to be slow in response to stimuli. So, for the first few months of their life they are naturally slow.

The Sensitive Infant Response

Depending on the state of their body [nervous system] and the levels of chemicals in them at birth, a person can be birthed with a sensitive infant response. This means that a person can be birthed with a tendency to be sensitive in response to stimuli. So, for the first few months of their life they are naturally sensitive.

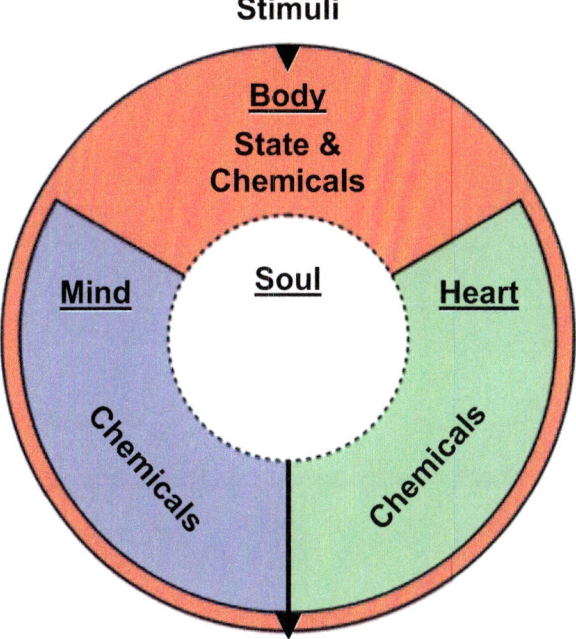

Chapter 4

THE THREE ESSENTIAL FACTORS

Since there are three processing parts to a person, there are three essential factors for a person to have the competence to be just, kind and right. The three essential factors are:

The mind sufficiency factor
The heart sufficiency factor
The body sufficiency factor

The Mind Sufficiency Factor

For a person to have the competence to be just, kind and right, they must have sufficient truthful opinions. This means that they must have sufficient truthful opinions formed in their mind by enough truthful knowledge. So, from birth to maturity a person must have enough truthful knowledge infused into their mind by it being told to them.

The Heart Sufficiency Factor

For a person to have the competence to be just, kind and right, they must have sufficient gracious cares. This means that they must have sufficient gracious cares formed in their heart by enough gracious understanding. So, from birth to maturity a person must have enough gracious understanding instructed into their heart by it being demonstrated and explained to them.

The Body Sufficiency Factor

For a person to have the competence to be just, kind and right, they must have sufficient righteous feelings. This means that they must have sufficient righteous feelings formed in their body by enough righteous experience. So, from birth to maturity a person must have enough righteous experience instilled into their body by them practicing it.

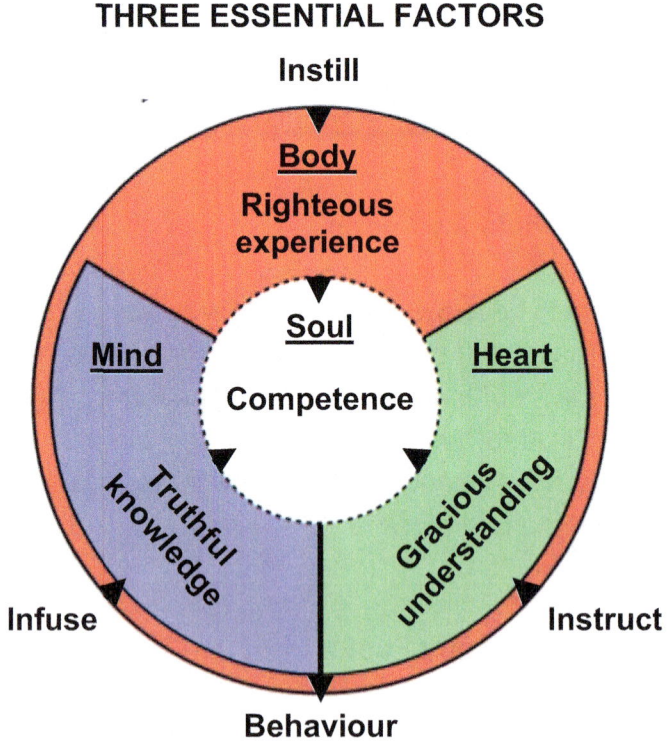

Chapter 5

THE THREE DETRIMENTAL FACTORS

Since there are three processing parts to a person, there are three detrimental factors to a person having the competence to be just, kind and right. The three detrimental factors are:

The mind insufficiency factor
The heart insufficiency factor
The body insufficiency factor

The Mind Insufficiency Factor

If a person has not had enough truthful knowledge infused into their mind by it being told to them, they will have insufficient truthful opinions. This means that they will not have enough truthful knowledge in their mind to have the competence to be just, kind and right. So, this person will have uncertainty [fear] regarding their behaviour.

The Heart Insufficiency Factor

If a person has not had enough gracious understanding instructed into their heart by it being demonstrated and explained to them, they will have insufficient gracious cares. This means that they will not have enough gracious understanding in their heart to have the competence to be just, kind and right. So, this person will have uncertainty [fear] regarding their behaviour.

The Body Insufficiency Factor

If a person has not had enough righteous experience instilled into their body by them practicing it, they will have insufficient righteous feelings. This means that they will have too much unrighteous experience in their body to have the competence to be just, kind and right. So, this person will have uncertainty [fear] regarding their behaviour.

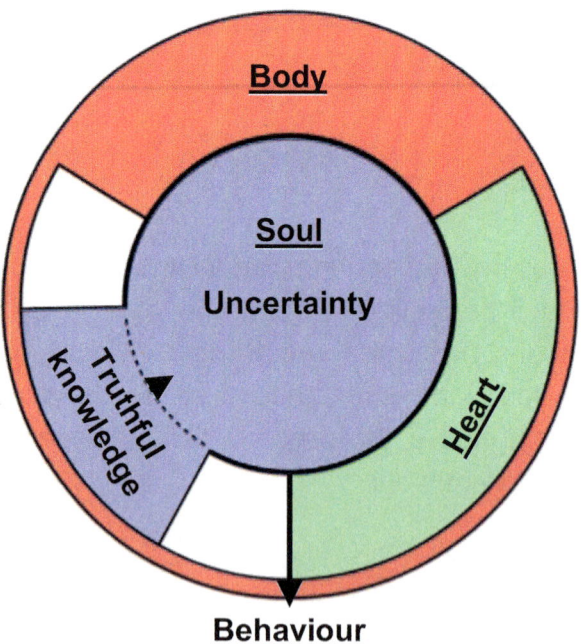

HEART INSUFFICIENCY FACTOR

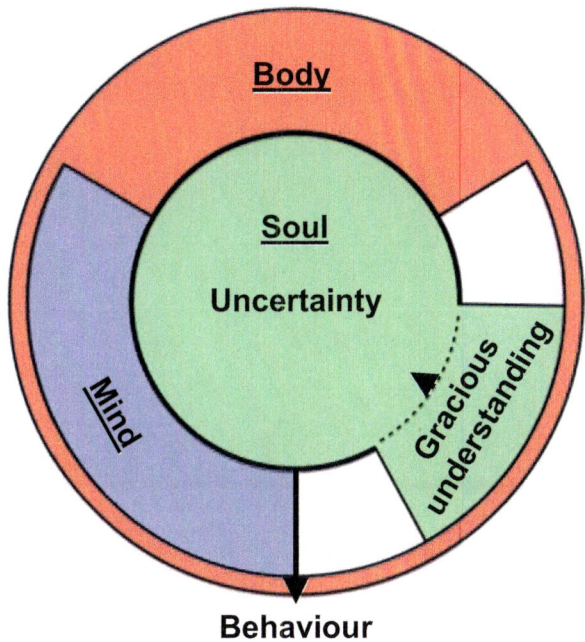

BODY INSUFFICIENCY FACTOR

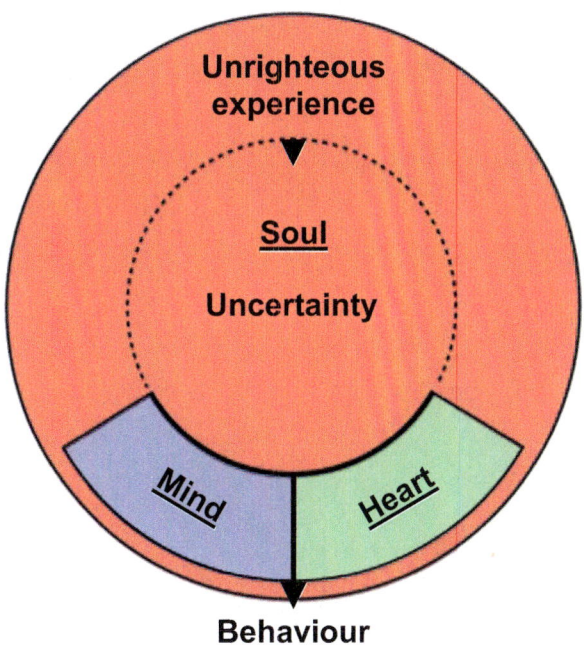

Chapter 6

THE FOUR CONSIDERATION METHODS

Since there are three processing parts and one information managing part to a person, a person can have one of four consideration methods. The four consideration methods are:

The non-biased consideration method
The mind-biased consideration method
The heart-biased consideration method
The body-biased consideration method

The Non-Biased Consideration Method

A person who has had enough truthful knowledge infused into their mind, enough gracious understanding instructed into their heart, and enough righteous experience instilled into their body, will typically equally consider the information from their sufficient truthful knowledge in their mind, their sufficient gracious understanding in their heart, and their sufficient righteous experience in their body. This means that they have a non-biased consideration method. So, this person will have the competence to be just, kind, and right, towards some people.

The Mind-Biased Consideration Method

A person who has not had enough truthful knowledge infused into their mind, will typically overly consider the information from their insufficient truthful knowledge in their mind, and give little or no consideration to gracious understanding in their heart or righteous experience in their body. This means that they have a mind-biased consideration method. So, this person will not have the competence to be just, kind, and right, towards any person. Instead, they will have uncertainty [fear] regarding their behaviour.

The Heart-Biased Consideration Method

A person who has not had enough gracious understanding instructed into their heart, will typically overly consider the information from their insufficient gracious understanding in their heart, and give little or no consideration to righteous experience in their body or truthful knowledge in their mind. This means that they have a heart-biased consideration method. So, this person will not have the competence to be just, kind, and right, towards any person. Instead, they will have uncertainty [fear] regarding their behaviour.

The Body-Biased Consideration Method

A person who has not had enough righteous experience instilled into their body, will typically overly consider the information from their excess unrighteous experience in their body, and give little or no consideration to truthful knowledge in their mind or gracious understanding in their heart. This means that they have a body-biased consideration method. So, this person will not have the competence to be just, kind, and right, towards any person. Instead, they will have uncertainty [fear] regarding their behaviour.

NON-BIASED CONSIDERATION METHOD

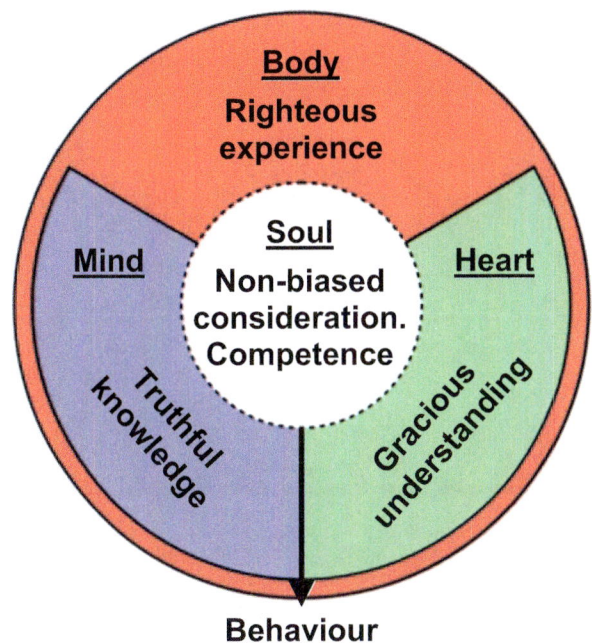

MIND-BIASED CONSIDERATION METHOD

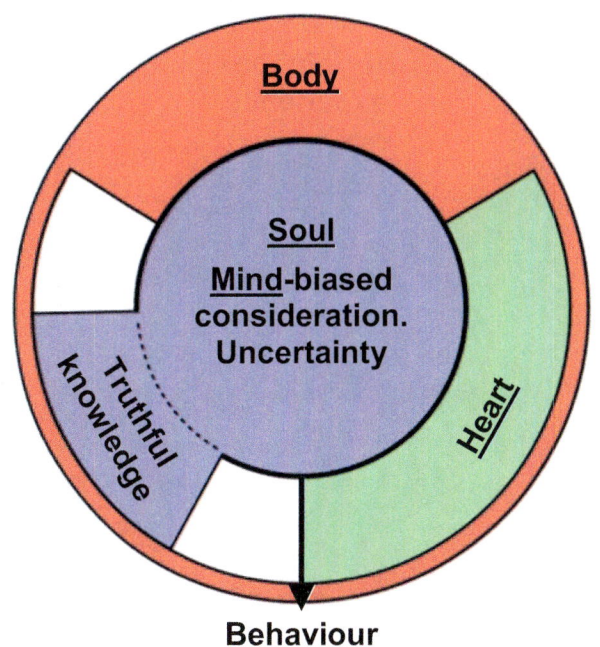

HEART-BIASED CONSIDERATION METHOD

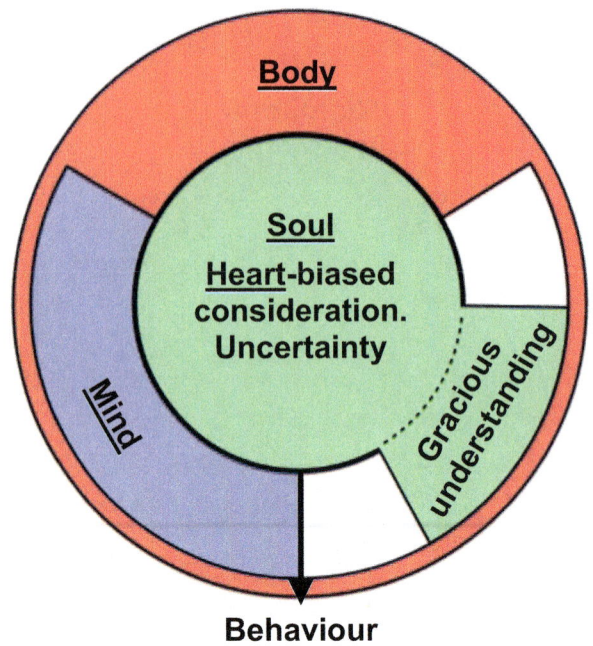

BODY-BIASED CONSIDERATION METHOD

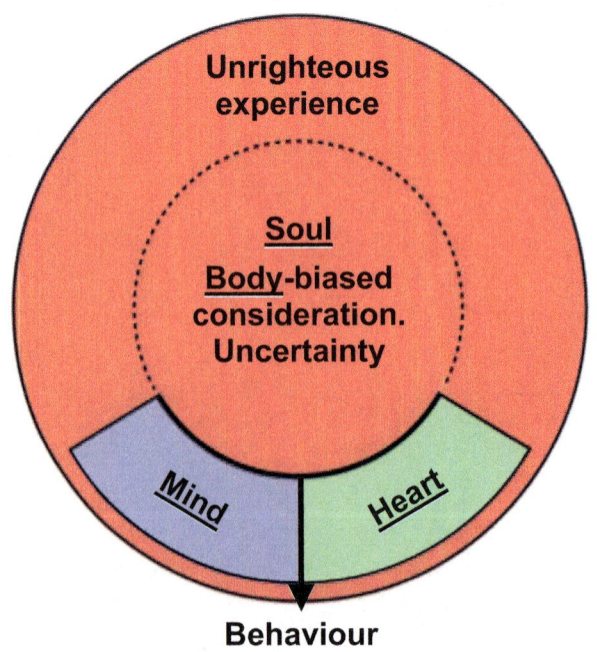

Chapter 7

THE FOUR PERSON TYPES

Since there are four consideration methods, there are four person types. Prov 1:5 & 22 [KJV]. The four person types are:

The non-biased person type
The mind-biased person type
The heart-biased person type
The body-biased person type

The Non-Biased Person Type

A person who has a non-biased consideration method, will typically equally consider the information from their sufficient truthful knowledge in their mind, their sufficient gracious understanding in their heart, and their sufficient righteous experience in their body, in order to decide how they will behave. This means that they are a non-biased person type. So, this person will be wise.

The Mind-Biased Person Type

A person who has a mind-biased consideration method, will typically overly consider the information from their insufficient truthful knowledge in their mind, and give little or no consideration to gracious understanding in their heart or righteous experience in their body, in order to decide how they will behave. This means that they are a mind-biased person type.

So, this person will be a fool.

The Heart-Biased Person Type

A person who has a heart-biased consideration method, will typically overly consider the information from their insufficient gracious understanding in their heart, and give little or no consideration to righteous experience in their body or truthful knowledge in their mind, in order to decide how they will behave. This means that they are a heart-biased person type. So, this person will be simple.

The Body-Biased Person Type

A person who has a body-biased consideration method, will typically overly consider the information from their excess unrighteous experience in their body, and give little or no consideration to truthful knowledge in their mind or gracious understanding in their heart, in order to decide how they will behave. This means that they are a body-biased person type. So, this person will be a scorner.

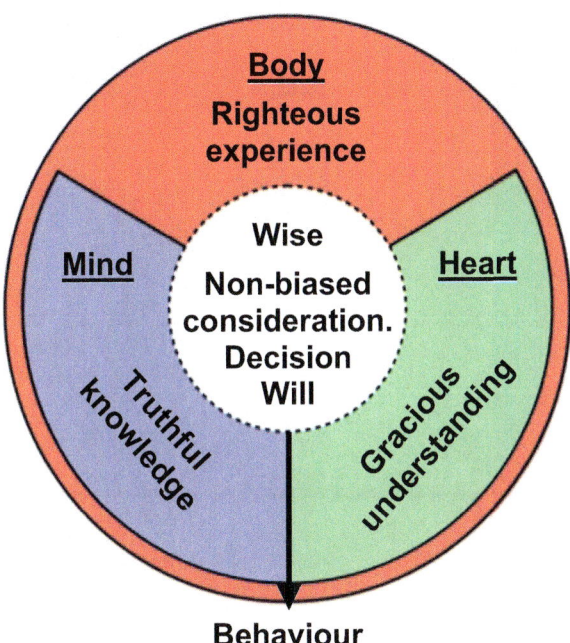

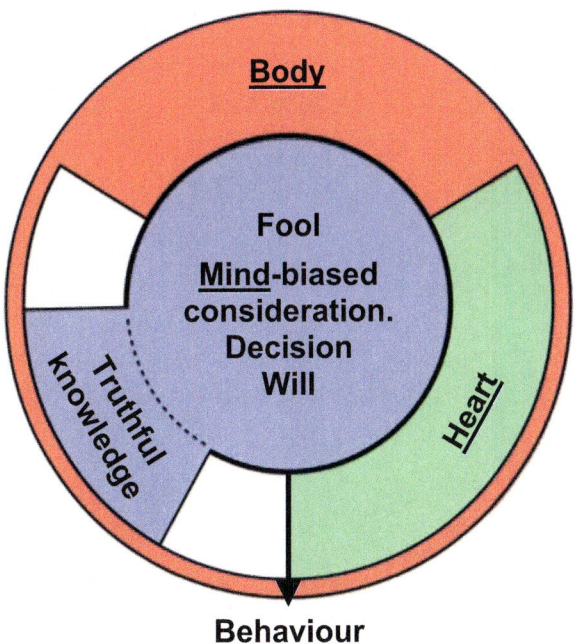

HEART-BIASED PERSON TYPE

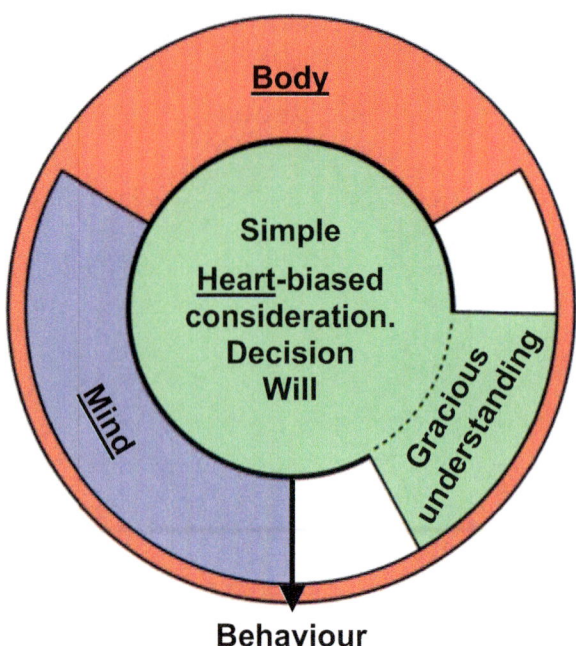

BODY-BIASED PERSON TYPE

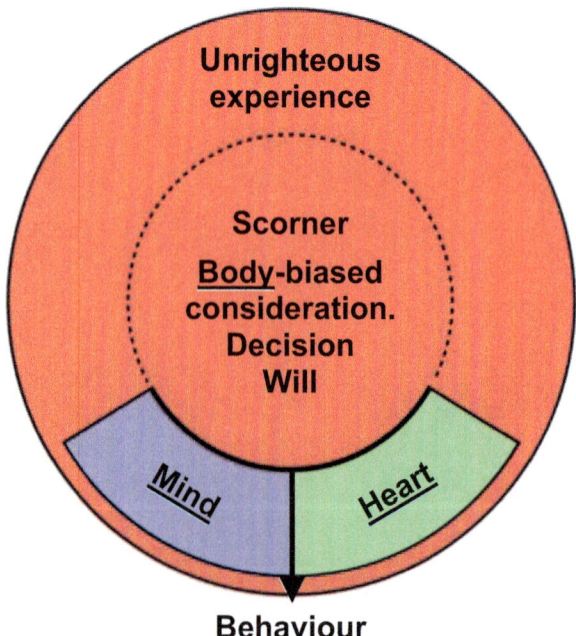

Chapter 8

THE FOUR LOVE LANGUAGES

Since there are four person types, there are four love languages. The four love languages are:

The non-biased love language
The mind-biased love language
The heart-biased love language
The body-biased love language

The Non-Biased Love Language

A non-biased person will have a non-biased love language. This means that they will typically equally consider the information from their sufficient truthful knowledge in their mind, their sufficient gracious understanding in their heart, and their sufficient righteous experience in their body, regarding how they express love. So, this person will equally consider assuring touch, mindful listening, helpful service, personal gifts, exclusive attention and praising words, as expressions of love.

The Mind-Biased Love Language

A mind-biased person will have a mind-biased love language. This means that they will typically overly consider the information from their insufficient truthful knowledge in their mind, and give little or no consideration to gracious understanding in their heart or righteous experience in their body, regarding how they express love. So, this person will overly consider assuring touch and mindful listening as expressions of love.

The Heart-Biased Love Language

A heart-biased person will have a heart-biased love language. This means that they will typically overly consider the information from their insufficient gracious understanding in their heart, and give little or no consideration to righteous experience in their body or truthful knowledge in their mind, regarding how they express love. So, this person will overly consider helpful service and personal gifts as expressions of love.

The Body-Biased Love Language

A body-biased person will have a body-biased love language. This means that they will typically overly consider the information from their excess unrighteous experience in their body, and give little or no consideration to truthful knowledge in their mind or gracious understanding in their heart, regarding how they express love. So, this person will overly consider exclusive attention and praising words as expressions of love.

NON-BIASED LOVE LANGUAGE

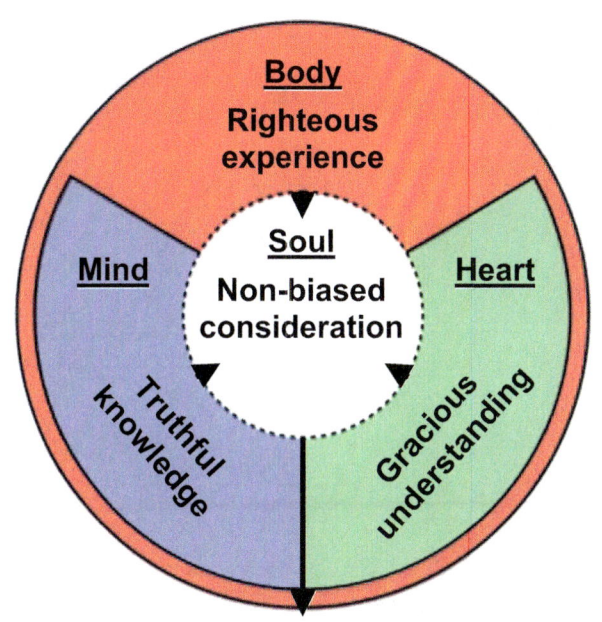

- **Body**: Righteous experience
- **Soul**: Non-biased consideration
- **Mind**: Truthful knowledge
- **Heart**: Gracious understanding

Touch, listening, service, gifts, attention & words

MIND-BIASED LOVE LANGUAGE

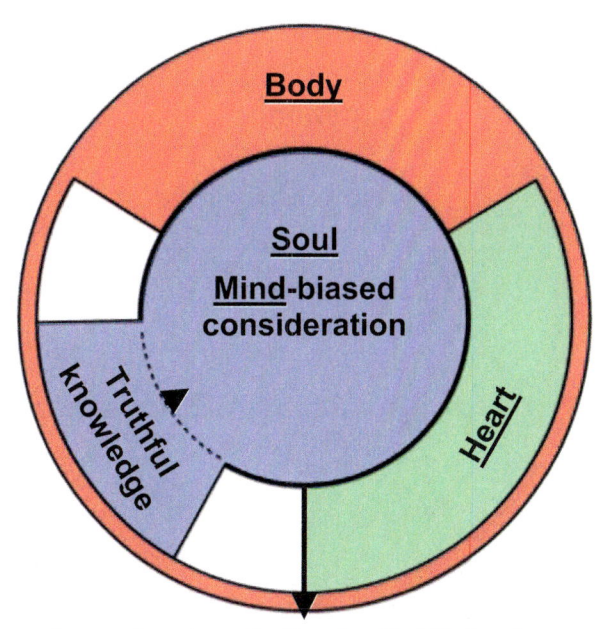

- **Body**
- **Soul**: Mind-biased consideration
- **Mind**: Truthful knowledge
- **Heart**

Assuring touch & mindful listening

HEART-BIASED LOVE LANGUAGE

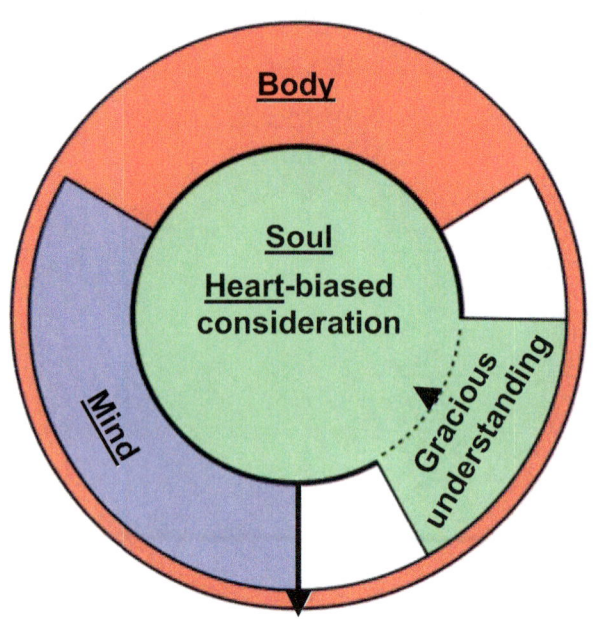

Body

Soul
Heart-biased consideration

Mind

Gracious understanding

Helpful service & personal gifts

BODY-BIASED LOVE LANGUAGE

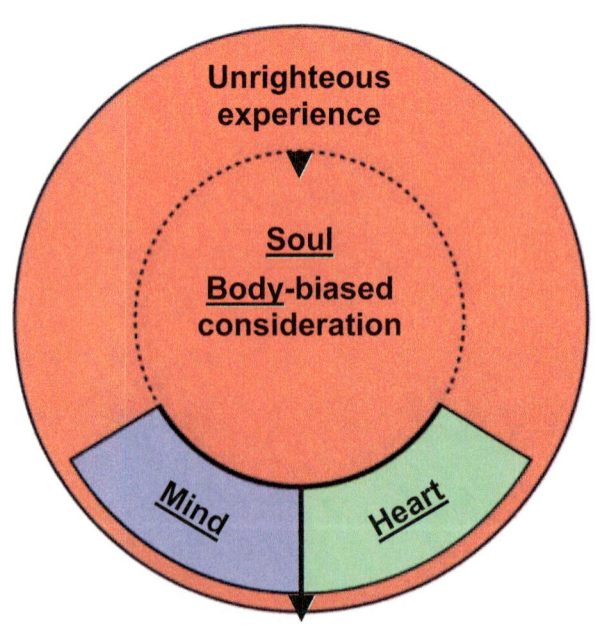

Unrighteous experience

Soul
Body-biased consideration

Mind

Heart

Exclusive attention & praising words

Chapter 9

THE FOUR ATTACHMENT STYLES

Since there are four person types, there are four attachment styles. The four attachment styles are:

The non-biased attachment style
The mind-biased attachment style
The heart-biased attachment style
The body-biased attachment style

The Non-Biased Attachment Style

A non-biased person will have a non-biased attachment style. This means that they will typically equally consider the information from their sufficient truthful knowledge in their mind, their sufficient gracious understanding in their heart, and their sufficient righteous experience in their body, regarding how they manage an attachment. So, this person will be competent in managing an attachment.

The Mind-Biased Attachment Style

A mind-biased person will have a mind-biased attachment style. This means that they will typically overly consider the information from their insufficient truthful knowledge in their mind, and give little or no consideration to gracious understanding in their heart or righteous experience in their body, regarding how they manage an attachment. So, this person will be anxious in managing an attachment.

The Heart-Biased Attachment Style

A heart-biased person will have a heart-biased attachment style. This means that they will typically overly consider the information from their insufficient gracious understanding in their heart, and give little or no consideration to righteous experience in their body or truthful knowledge in their mind, regarding how they manage an attachment. So, this person will be overcaring in managing an attachment.

The Body-Biased Attachment Style

A body-biased person will have a body-biased attachment style. This means that they will typically overly consider the information from their excess unrighteous experience in their body, and give little or no consideration to truthful knowledge in their mind or gracious understanding in their heart, regarding how they manage an attachment. So, this person will be stressed in managing an attachment.

NON-BIASED ATTACHMENT STYLE

- **Body**: Righteous experience
- **Soul**: Non-biased consideration
- **Mind**: Truthful knowledge
- **Heart**: Gracious understanding

Competent

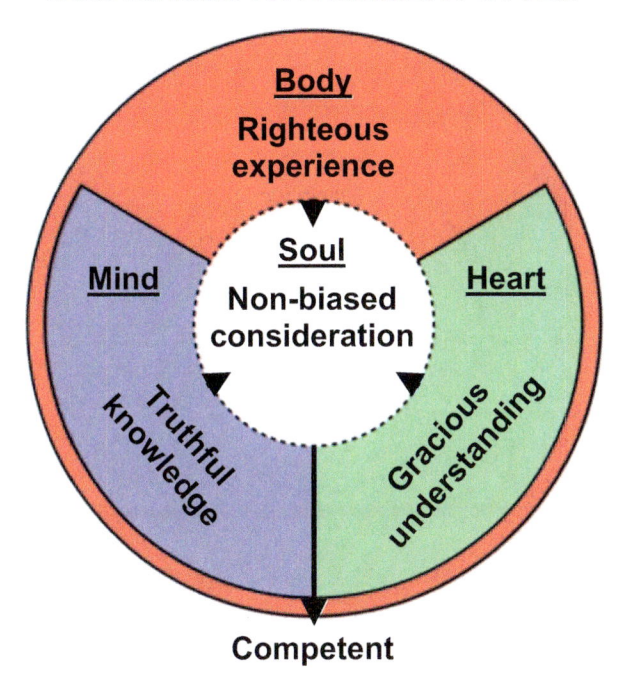

MIND-BIASED ATTACHMENT STYLE

- **Body**
- **Soul**: Mind-biased consideration
- **Heart**
- Truthful knowledge

Anxious

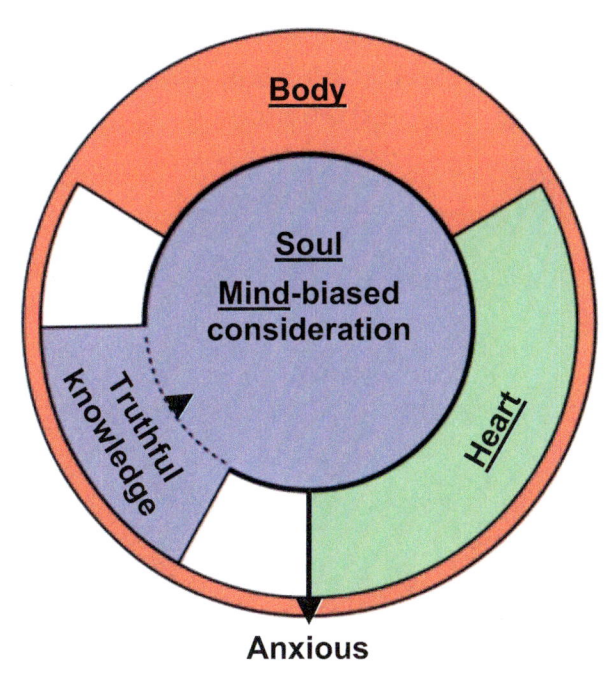

HEART-BIASED ATTACHMENT STYLE

- Body
- Soul
- **Heart**-biased consideration
- Mind
- Gracious understanding
- Overcaring

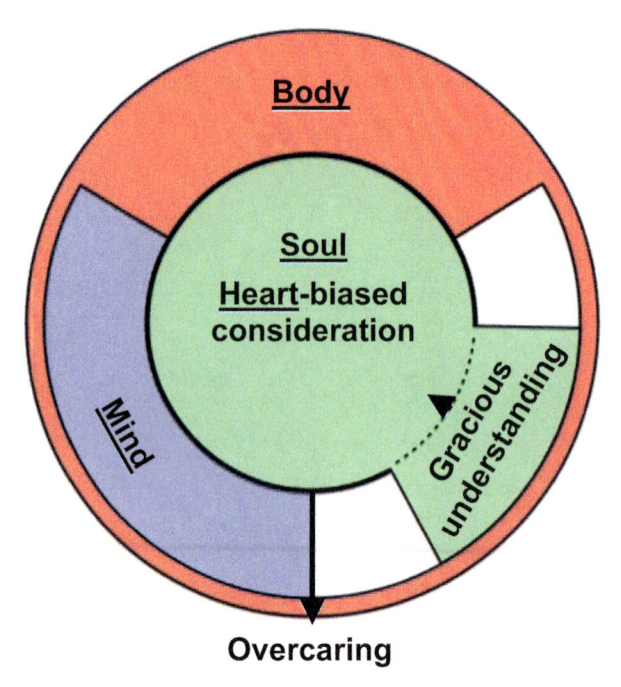

BODY-BIASED ATTACHMENT STYLE

- Unrighteous experience
- Soul
- **Body**-biased consideration
- Mind
- Heart
- Stressed

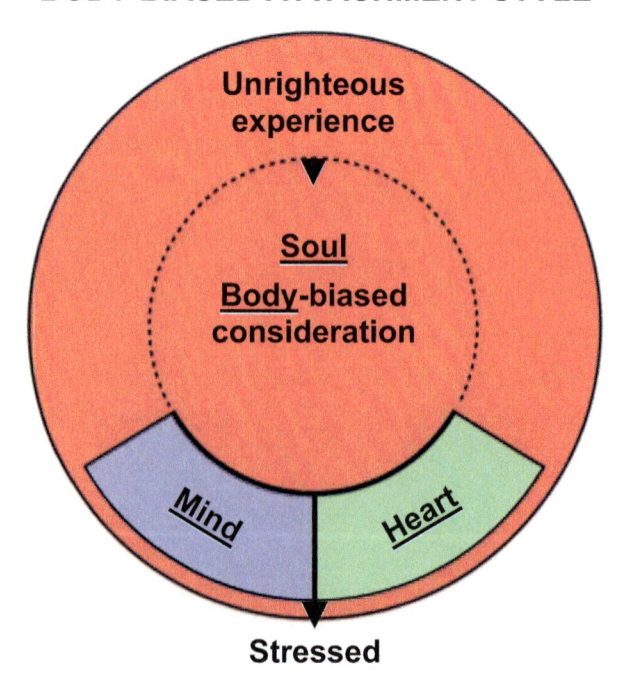

Chapter 10

THE FOUR RESPONSES TO GOD'S WORD

Since there are four person types, there are four responses to God's Word. Mk 4:13-20 [KJV]. The four responses are:

The non-biased response to God's Word
The mind-biased response to God's Word
The heart-biased response to God's Word
The body-biased response to God's Word

The Non-Biased Response to God's Word

A non-biased person will have a non-biased response to God's Word. This means that they will typically equally consider the information from their sufficient truthful knowledge in their mind, their sufficient gracious understanding in their heart, and their sufficient righteous experience in their body, regarding God's call for repentance. Lk 5:32 [KJV]. So, this person [good ground] will whole-heartedly accept truth from the Bible.

The Mind-Biased Response to God's Word

A mind-biased person will have a mind-biased response to God's Word. This means that they will typically overly consider the information from their insufficient truthful knowledge in their mind, and give little or no consideration to gracious understanding in their heart or righteous experience in their body, regarding God's call for repentance. So, this person [stony ground] will shallow-heartedly accept truth from the Bible.

The Heart-Biased Response to God's Word

A heart-biased person will have a heart-biased response to God's Word. This means that they will typically overly consider the information from their insufficient gracious understanding in their heart, and give little or no consideration to righteous experience in their body or truthful knowledge in their mind, regarding God's call for repentance. So, this person [thorny ground] will half-heartedly accept truth from the Bible.

The Body-Biased Response to God's Word

A body-biased person will have a body-biased response to God's Word. This means that they will typically overly consider the information from their excess unrighteous experience in their body, and give little or no consideration to truthful knowledge in their mind or gracious understanding in their heart, regarding God's call for repentance. So, this person [wayside] will hard-heartedly refuse to accept truth from the Bible.

NON-BIASED RESPONSE TO GOD'S WORD

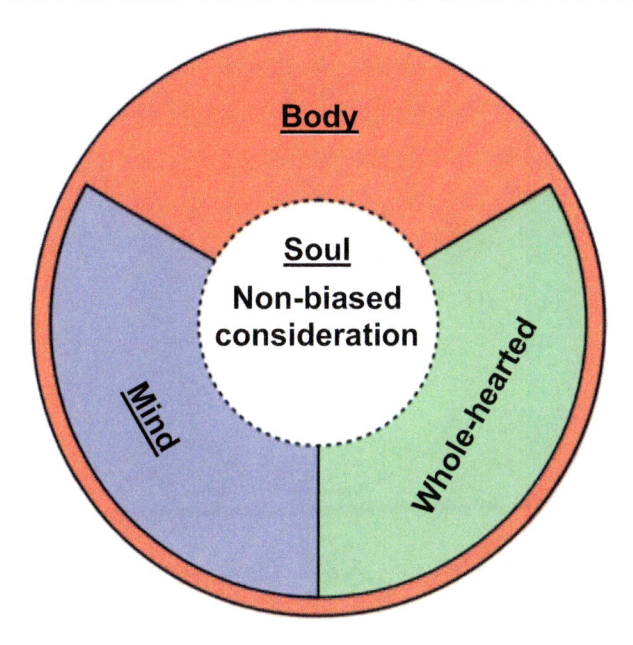

- Body
- Soul: Non-biased consideration
- Mind
- Whole-hearted

MIND-BIASED RESPONSE TO GOD'S WORD

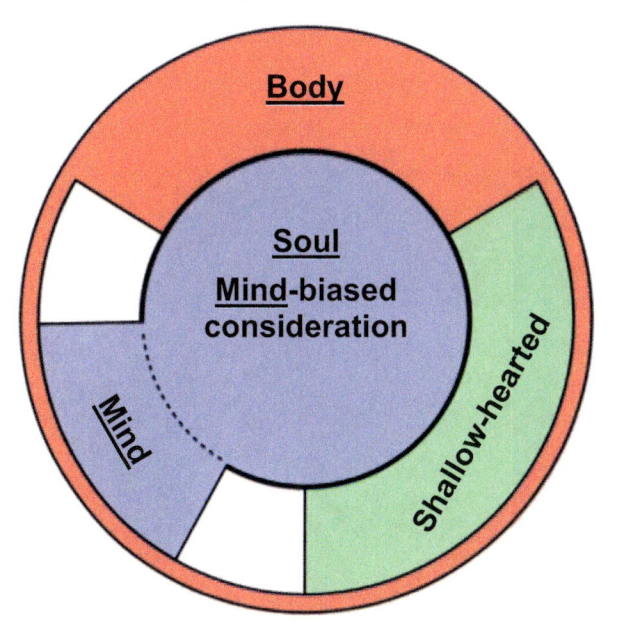

- Body
- Soul: Mind-biased consideration
- Mind
- Shallow-hearted

HEART-BIASED RESPONSE TO GOD'S WORD

- Body
- Soul: **Heart**-biased consideration
- Mind
- Half-hearted

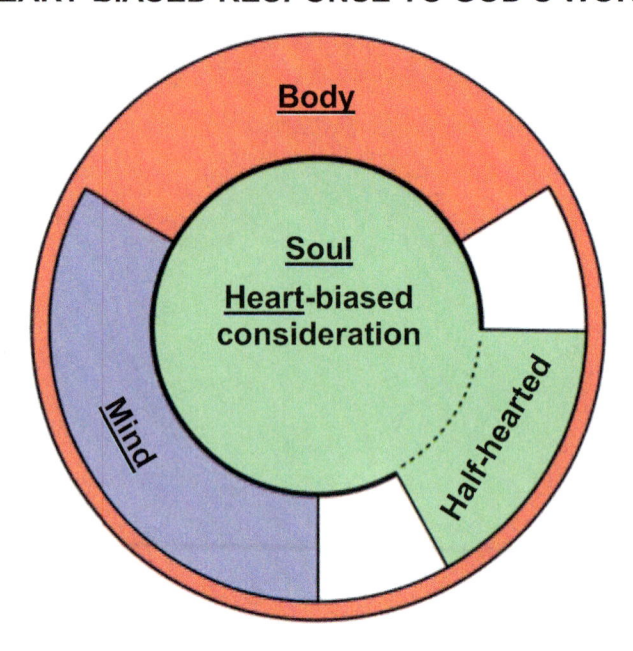

BODY-BIASED RESPONSE TO GOD'S WORD

- Body
- Soul: **Body**-biased consideration
- Mind
- Hard-hearted

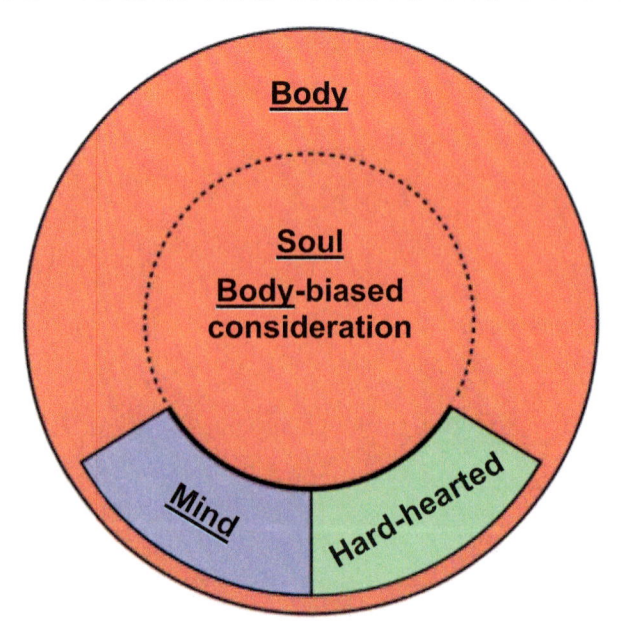

Chapter 11

THE FOUR BELIEFS IN GOD'S WORD

Since there are four responses to God's Word, there are four beliefs in God's Word. The four beliefs are:

The non-biased belief in God's Word
The mind-biased belief in God's Word
The heart-biased belief in God's Word
The body-biased belief in God's Word

The Non-Biased Belief in God's Word

A non-biased person will have a non-biased belief in God's Word. This means that they will typically equally consider the information from their sufficient truthful knowledge in their mind, their sufficient gracious understanding in their heart, and their sufficient righteous experience in their body, regarding God's command to be just, kind, and right, towards all people. Matt 5:43-48; Lk 6:31-35 [KJV]. So, this person, having wholeheartedly accepted truth from the Bible, will become a faithful believer.

The Mind-Biased Belief in God's Word

A mind-biased person will have a mind-biased belief in God's Word. This means that they will typically overly consider the information from their insufficient truthful knowledge in their mind, and give little or no consideration to gracious understanding in their heart or righteous experience in their body, regarding God's command to be just, kind, and right, towards all people. So, this person, having shallow-heartedly accepted truth from the Bible, will become a false believer.

The Heart-Biased Belief in God's Word

A heart-biased person will have a heart-biased belief in God's Word. This means that they will typically overly consider the information from their insufficient gracious understanding in their heart, and give little or no consideration to righteous experience in their body or truthful knowledge in their mind, regarding God's command to be just, kind, and right, towards all people. So, this person, having half-heartedly accepted truth from the Bible, will become an unfaithful believer.

The Body-Biased Belief in God's Word

A body-biased person will have a body-biased belief in God's Word. This means that they will typically overly consider the information from their excess unrighteous experience in their body, and give little or no consideration to truthful knowledge in their mind or gracious understanding in their heart, regarding God's command to be just, kind, and right, towards all people. So, this person, having hard-heartedly refused to accept truth from the Bible, will remain an unbeliever.

NON-BIASED BELIEF IN GOD'S WORD

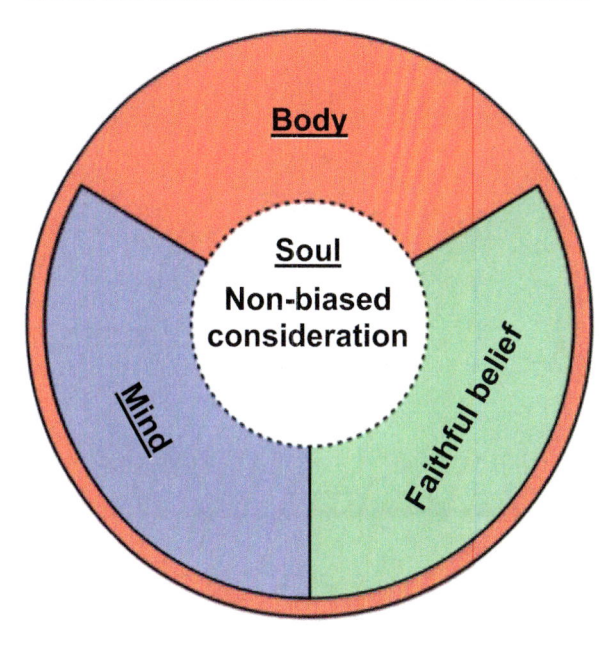

Body

Soul
Non-biased consideration

Mind

Faithful belief

MIND-BIASED BELIEF IN GOD'S WORD

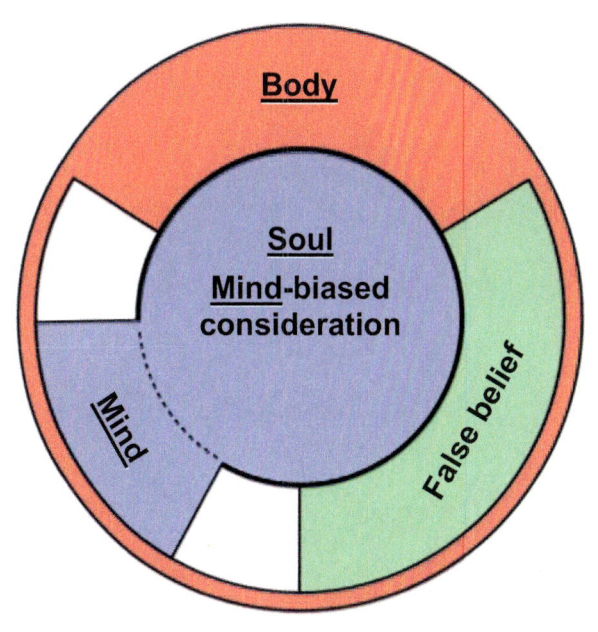

Body

Soul
Mind-biased consideration

Mind

False belief

HEART-BIASED BELIEF IN GOD'S WORD

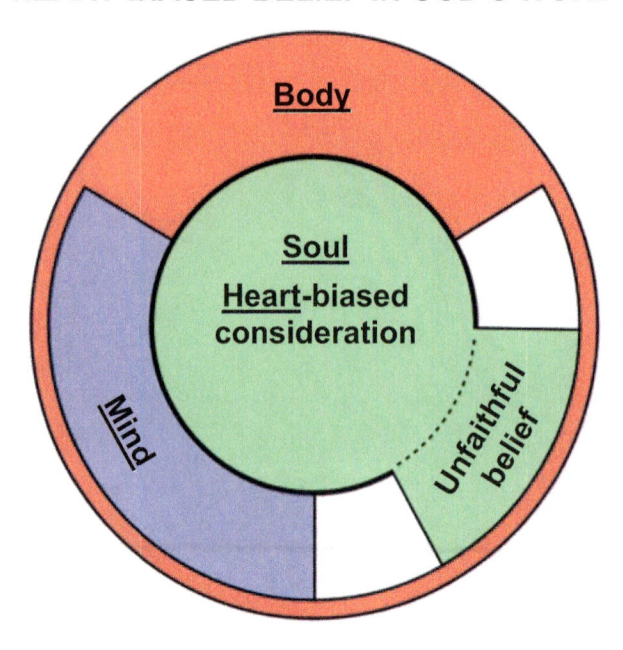

Body

Soul
Heart-biased consideration

Mind

Unfaithful belief

BODY-BIASED BELIEF IN GOD'S WORD

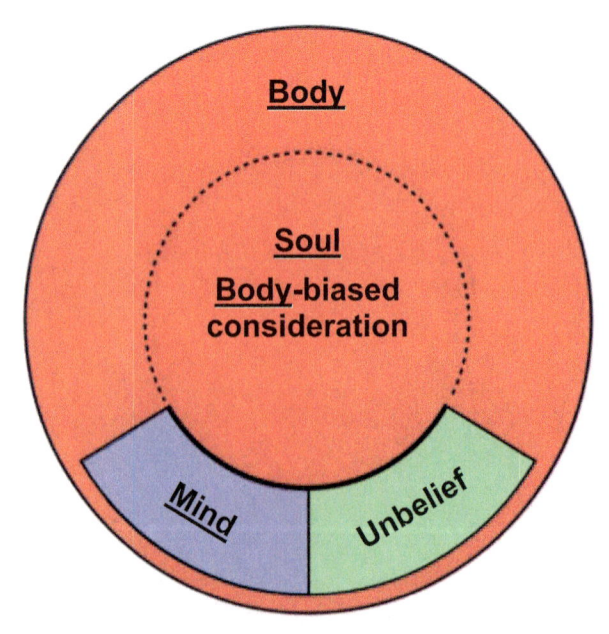

Body

Soul
Body-biased consideration

Mind

Unbelief

Chapter 12

THE FOUR NON-BIASED BEHAVIOUR STYLES

Since there is one non-biased person type and three processing parts to a person, there are four non-biased behaviour styles. The four non-biased behaviour styles are:

The non-dominant, non-biased behaviour style
The mind-dominant, non-biased behaviour style
The heart-dominant, non-biased behaviour style
The body-dominant, non-biased behaviour style

The Non-Dominant, Non-Biased Behaviour Style

A non-biased person can have a non-dominant, non-biased behaviour style. This means that their behaviour is typically equally governed by their sufficient truthful opinions in their mind, by their sufficient gracious cares in their heart, and by their sufficient righteous feelings in their body, while being illustrative of their equal consideration of their sufficient truthful knowledge in their mind, of their sufficient gracious understanding in their heart, and of their sufficient righteous experience in their body. So, this person will have an equally consultative, supportive and directive, wise behaviour style.

The Mind-Dominant, Non-Biased Behaviour Style

A non-biased person can have a mind-dominant, non-biased behaviour style. This means that their behaviour is typically dominated by their sufficient truthful opinions in their mind, while being illustrative of their equal consideration of their truthful knowledge in their mind, of their sufficient gracious understanding in their heart, and of their sufficient righteous experience in their body. So, this person will have a mostly consultative, wise behaviour style.

The Heart-Dominant, Non-Biased Behaviour Style

A non-biased person can have a heart-dominant, non-biased behaviour style. This means that their behaviour is typically dominated by their sufficient gracious cares in their heart, while being illustrative of their equal consideration of their sufficient truthful knowledge in their mind, of their sufficient gracious understanding in their heart, and of their sufficient righteous experience in their body. So, this person will have a mostly supportive, wise behaviour style.

The Body-Dominant, Non-Biased Behaviour Style

A non-biased person can have a body-dominant, non-biased behaviour style. This means that their behaviour is typically dominated by their sufficient righteous feelings in their body, while being illustrative of their equal consideration of their sufficient truthful knowledge in their mind, of their sufficient gracious understanding in their heart, and of their sufficient righteous experience in their body. So, this person will have a mostly directive, wise behaviour style.

NON-DOMINANT, NON-BIASED BEHAVIOUR STYLE

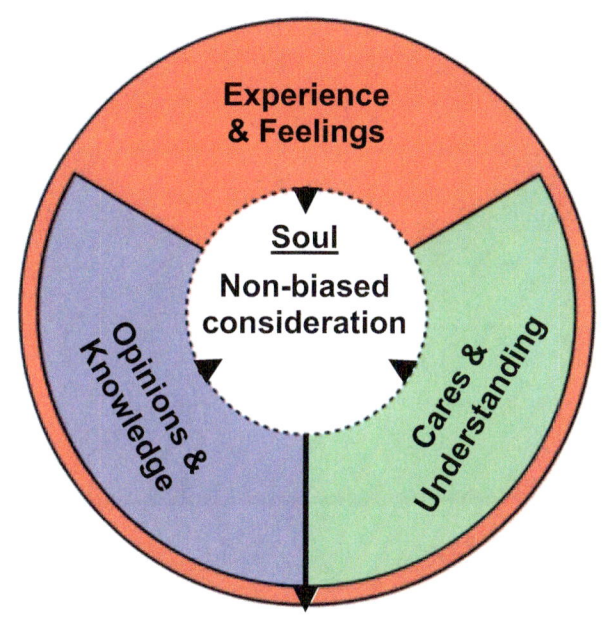

- Experience & Feelings
- Opinions & Knowledge
- Cares & Understanding

Soul
Non-biased consideration

Equally consultative, supportive & directive, wise

MIND-DOMINANT, NON-BIASED BEHAVIOUR STYLE

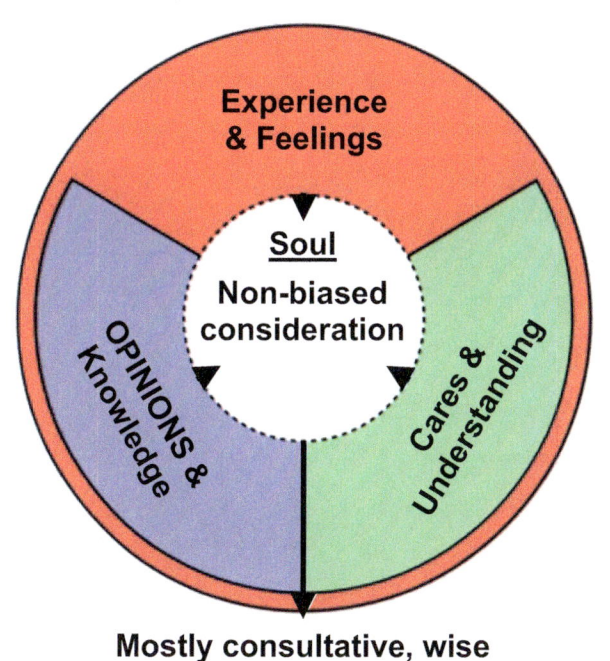

- Experience & Feelings
- OPINIONS & Knowledge
- Cares & Understanding

Soul
Non-biased consideration

Mostly consultative, wise

HEART-DOMINANT, NON-BIASED BEHAVIOUR STYLE

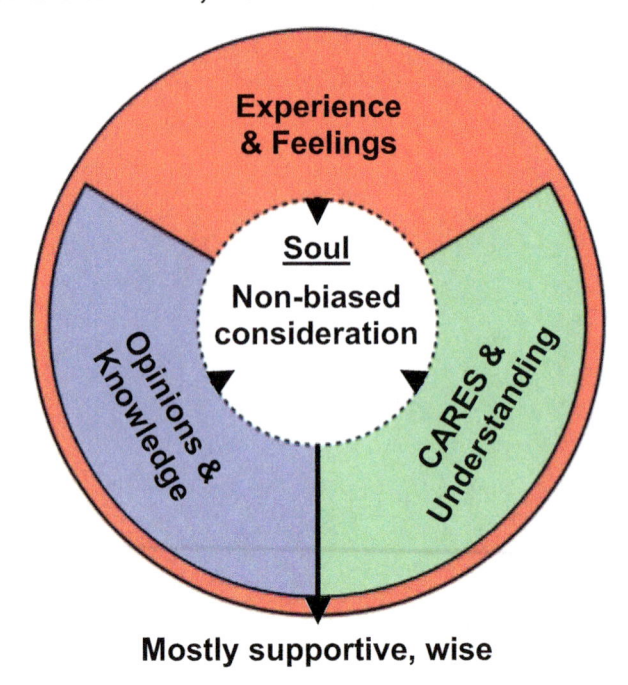

Experience & Feelings

Soul
Non-biased consideration

Opinions & Knowledge

CARES & Understanding

Mostly supportive, wise

BODY-DOMINANT, NON-BIASED BEHAVIOUR STYLE

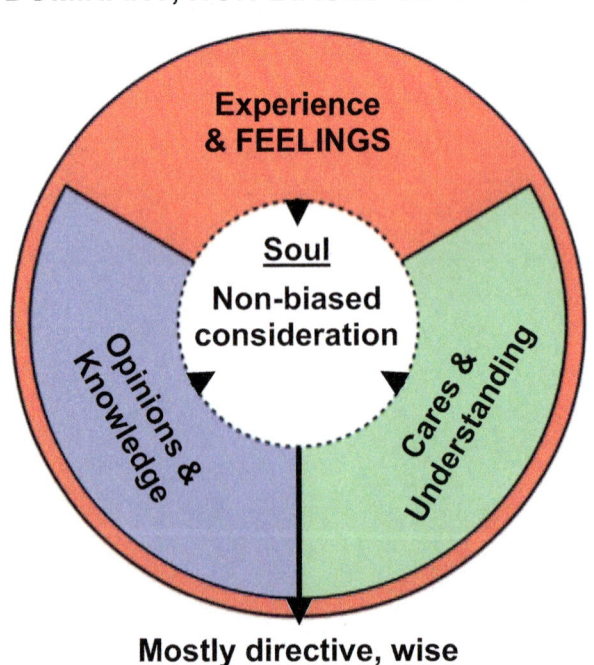

Experience & FEELINGS

Soul
Non-biased consideration

Opinions & Knowledge

Cares & Understanding

Mostly directive, wise

Chapter 13

THE TWO DEGREES OF BIAS

Since there are two degrees of psychological problems, which mainstream psychology has termed "mental, emotional and social disorders" and "personality disorders", there are two degrees of bias. The two degrees of bias are:

The distinct degree of bias
The extreme degree of bias

The Distinct Degree of Bias

A person can have a distinct psychological problem specifically with either their mind, their heart or their body [nervous system], which mainstream psychology has categorized as "mental, emotional and social disorders", respectively. This means that a person can have a distinct problem with either insufficient truthful opinions in their mind, insufficient gracious cares in their heart, or excessive unrighteous feelings in their body. So, a person can have a distinct degree of bias towards either their mind, heart or body.

The Extreme Degree of Bias

A person can have an extreme psychological problem specifically with either their mind, their heart or their body, which mainstream psychology has categorized as "clusters A, C and B personality disorders", respectively. This means that a person can have an extreme problem with either insufficient truthful opinions in their mind, insufficient gracious cares in their heart, or excessive unrighteous feelings in their body. So, a person can have an extreme degree of bias towards either their mind, heart or body.

DISTINCT MIND-BIASED CONSIDERATION

- Body
- Distinct **Mind**-biased consideration
- Mind
- Heart

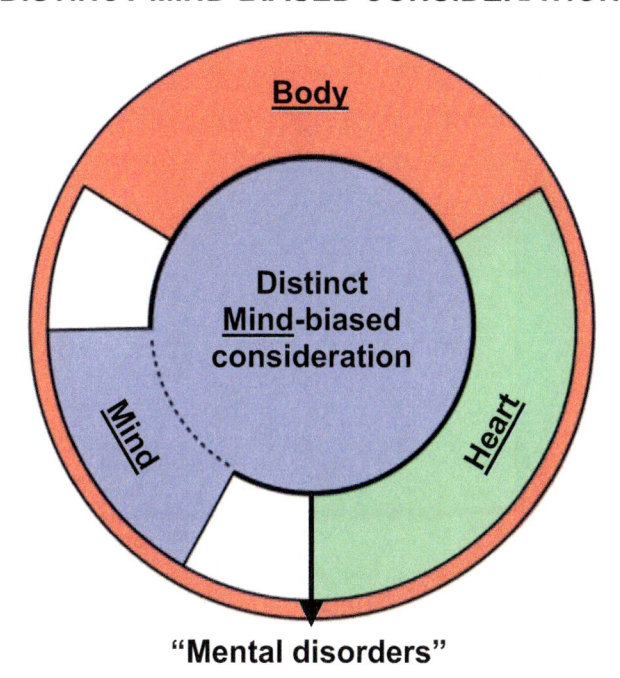

→ "Mental disorders"

EXTREME MIND-BIASED CONSIDERATION

- Body
- Extreme **Mind**-biased consideration
- Mind
- Heart

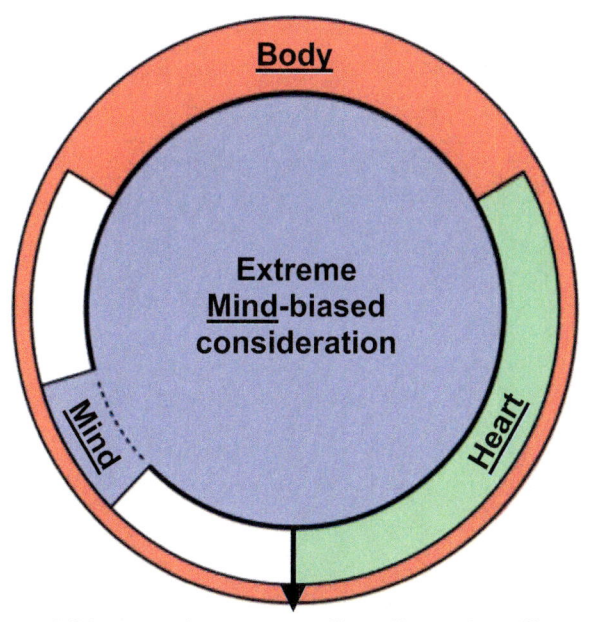

→ "Cluster A personality disorders"

DISTINCT HEART-BIASED CONSIDERATION

Body

Distinct Heart-biased consideration

Mind

Heart

↓

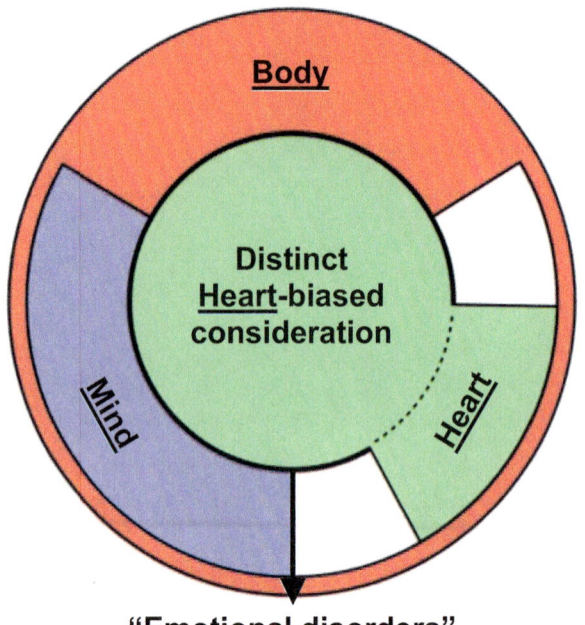

"Emotional disorders"

EXTREME HEART-BIASED CONSIDERATION

Body

Extreme Heart-biased consideration

Mind

Heart

↓

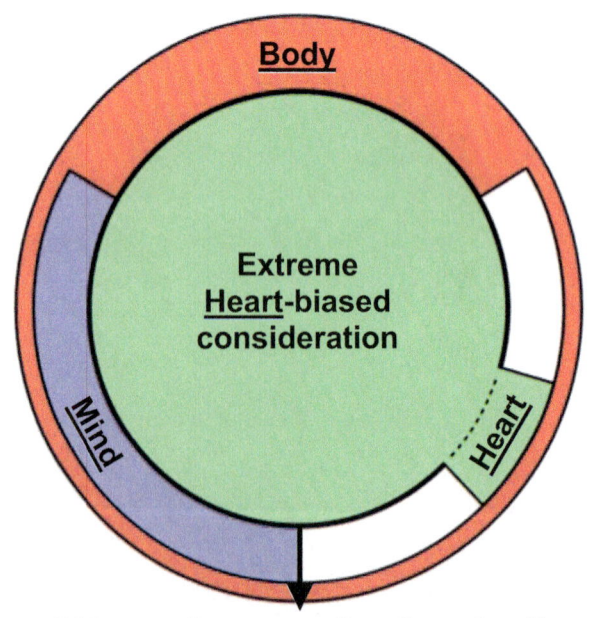

"Cluster C personality disorders"

DISTINCT BODY-BIASED CONSIDERATION

Body

Distinct **Body**-biased consideration

Mind | Heart

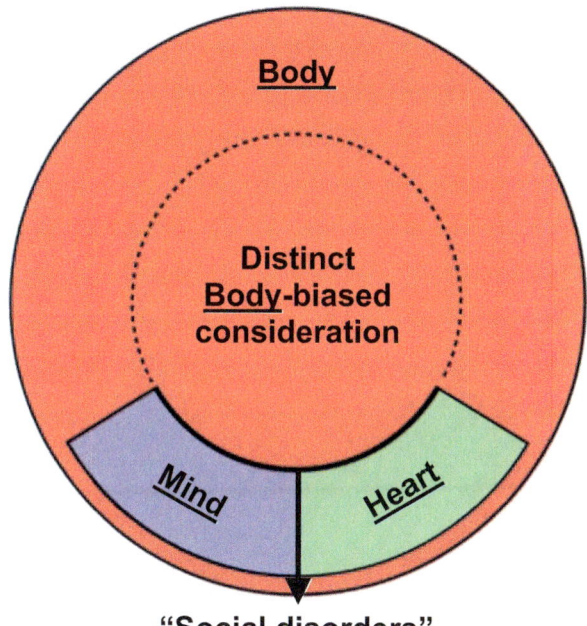

"Social disorders"

EXTREME BODY-BIASED CONSIDERATION

Body

Extreme **Body**-biased consideration

Mind | Heart

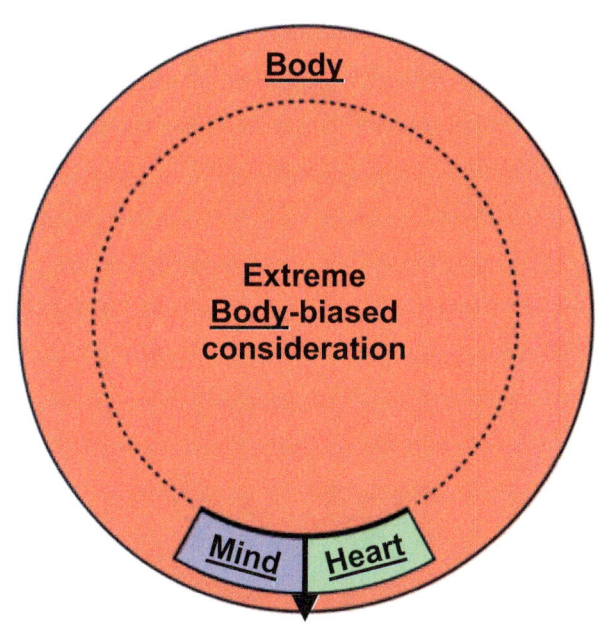

"Cluster B personality disorders"

Chapter 14

THE SIX
BIASED BEHAVIOUR STYLES

Since there are three biased person types and two degrees of bias, there are six biased behaviour styles. The six biased behaviour styles are:

The distinctly mind-biased behaviour style
The extremely mind-biased behaviour style
The distinctly heart-biased behaviour style
The extremely heart-biased behaviour style
The distinctly body-biased behaviour style
The extremely body-biased behaviour style

The Distinctly Mind-Biased Behaviour Style

A distinctly mind-biased person will have a distinctly mind-biased behaviour style. This means that their behaviour is typically determined by their insufficient truthful opinions in their mind, and illustrative of their distinct over consideration of their insufficient truthful knowledge in their mind, and their distinct inconsideration of any gracious understanding in their heart or righteous experience in their body. So, this person will have a passive and foolish behaviour style.

The Extremely Mind-Biased Behaviour Style

An extremely mind-biased person will have an extremely mind-biased behaviour style. This means that their behaviour is typically determined by their insufficient truthful opinions in their mind, and illustrative of their extreme over consideration of their insufficient truthful knowledge in their mind, and their extreme inconsideration of any gracious understanding in their heart or righteous experience in their body. So this person will have a withdrawn and paranoid behaviour style.

The Distinctly Heart-Biased Behaviour Style

A distinctly heart-biased person will have a distinctly heart-biased behaviour style. This means that their behaviour is typically determined by their insufficient gracious cares in their heart, and illustrative of their distinct over consideration of their insufficient gracious understanding in their heart, and their distinct inconsideration of any righteous experience in their body or truthful knowledge in their mind. So, this person will have a subservient and naive behaviour style.

The Extremely Heart-Biased Behaviour Style

An extremely heart-biased person will have an extremely heart-biased behaviour style. This means that their behaviour is typically determined by their insufficient gracious cares in their heart, and illustrative of their extreme over consideration of their insufficient gracious understanding in their heart, and their extreme inconsideration of any righteous experience in their body or truthful knowledge in their mind. So, this person will have a reserved and dependent behaviour style

The Distinctly Body-Biased Behaviour Style

A distinctly body-biased person will have a distinctly body-biased behaviour style. This means that their behaviour is typically determined by their excess unrighteous feelings in their body, and illustrative of their distinct over consideration of their excess unrighteous experience in their body, and their distinct inconsideration of any truthful knowledge in their mind or gracious understanding in their heart. So, this person will have a manipulative and contemptuous behaviour style.

The Extremely Body-Biased Behaviour Style

An extremely body-biased person will have an extremely body-biased behaviour style. This means that their behaviour is typically determined by their excess unrighteous feelings in their body, and illustrative of their extreme over consideration of their excess unrighteous experience in their body, and their extreme inconsideration of any truthful knowledge in their mind or gracious understanding in their heart. So, this person will have a domineering and narcissistic behaviour style.

DISTINCTLY MIND-BIASED BEHAVIOUR STYLE

Body / **Heart** / Distinct **Mind**-biased consideration / Opinions & Knowledge

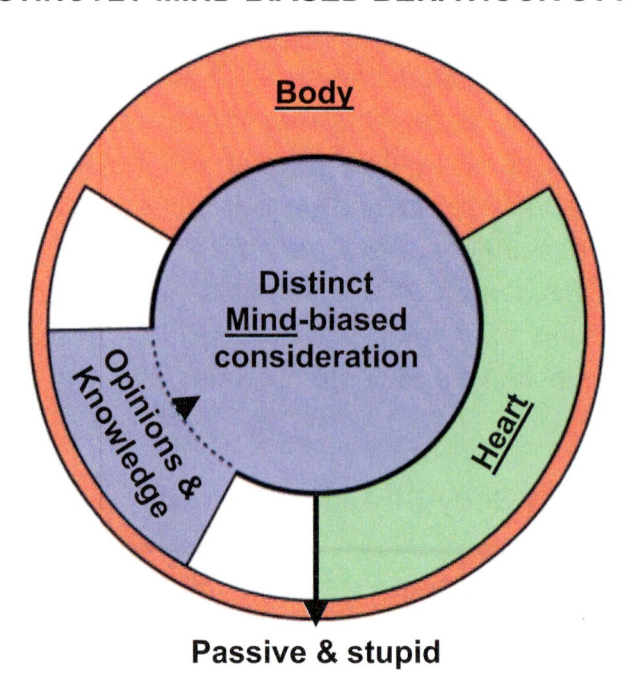

Passive & stupid

EXTREMELY MIND-BIASED BEHAVIOUR STYLE

Body / **Heart** / Extreme **Mind**-biased consideration / O & K

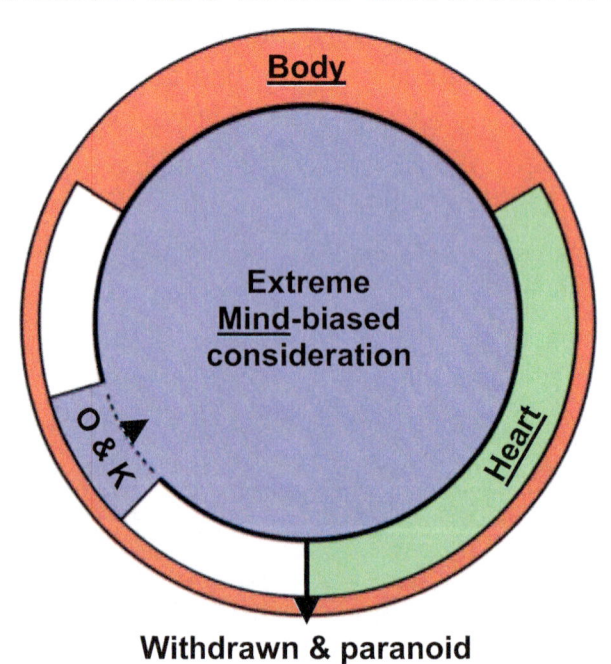

Withdrawn & paranoid

DISTINCTLY HEART-BIASED BEHAVIOUR STYLE

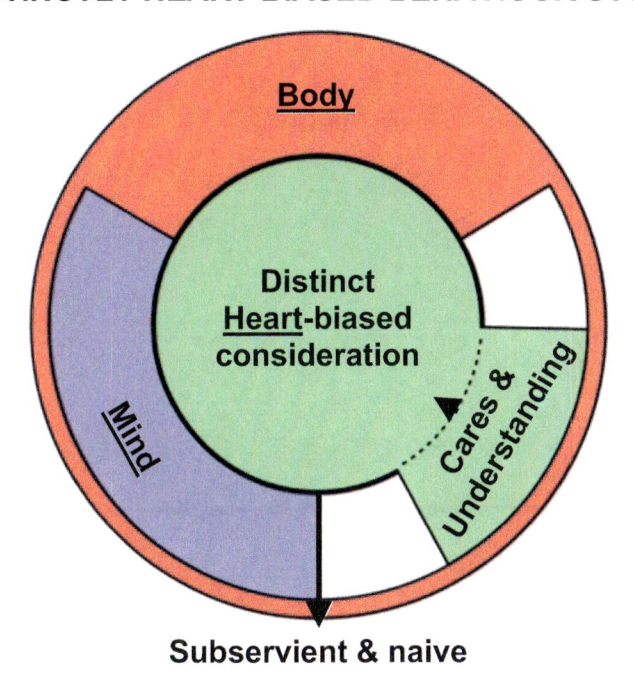

Body

Distinct *Heart*-biased consideration

Cares & Understanding

Mind

Subservient & naive

EXTREMELY HEART-BIASED BEHAVIOUR STYLE

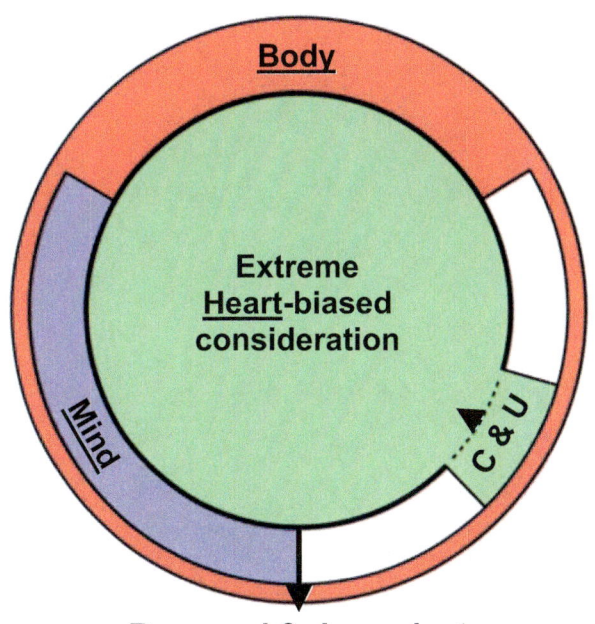

Body

Extreme *Heart*-biased consideration

C & U

Mind

Reserved & dependent

DISTINCTLY BODY-BIASED BEHAVIOUR STYLE

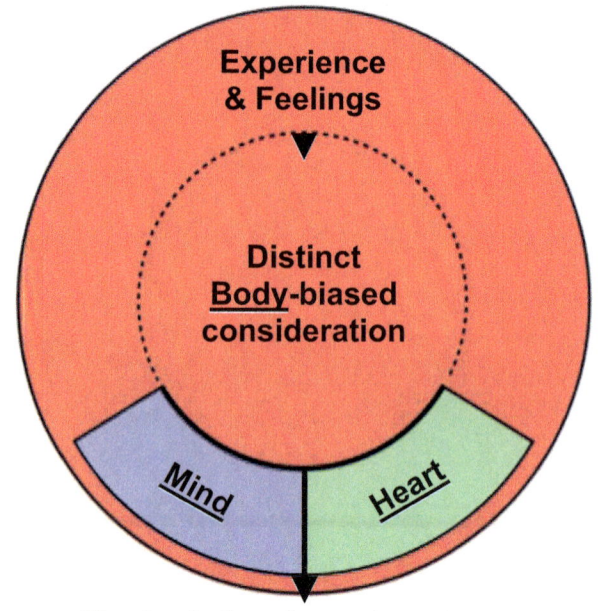

Experience & Feelings

Distinct Body-biased consideration

Mind *Heart*

Manipulative & contemptuous

EXTREMELY BODY-BIASED BEHAVIOUR STYLE

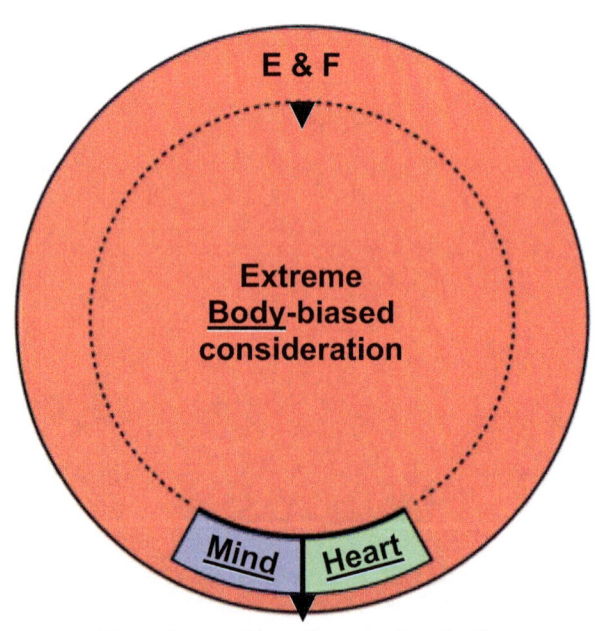

E & F

Extreme Body-biased consideration

Mind *Heart*

Domineering & narcissistic

Chapter 15

THE THREE BIAS PROBLEMS

Since there are three biased person types, there are three bias problems. The three bias problems are:

The mind-biased consideration
The heart-biased consideration
The body-biased consideration

The Mind-Biased Consideration

A mind-biased person has a mind-biased consideration. This means that they overly consider the insufficient truthful knowledge in their mind, and give little or no consideration to any gracious understanding in their heart or righteous experience in their body. So, this person will not have the competence to be just, kind, and right, towards any person. Instead, they will have uncertainty [fear] regarding their behaviour.

The Heart-Biased Consideration

A heart-biased person has a heart-biased consideration. This means that they overly consider the insufficient gracious understanding in their heart, and give little or no consideration to any righteous experience in their body or truthful knowledge in their mind. So, this person will not have the competence to be just, kind, and right, towards any person. Instead, they will have uncertainty [fear] regarding their behaviour.

The Body-Biased Consideration

A body-biased person has a body-biased consideration. This means that they overly consider the excess unrighteous experience in their body, and give little or no consideration to any truthful knowledge in their mind or gracious understanding in their heart. So, this person will not have the competence to be just, kind, and right, towards any person. Instead, they will have uncertainty [fear] regarding their behaviour.

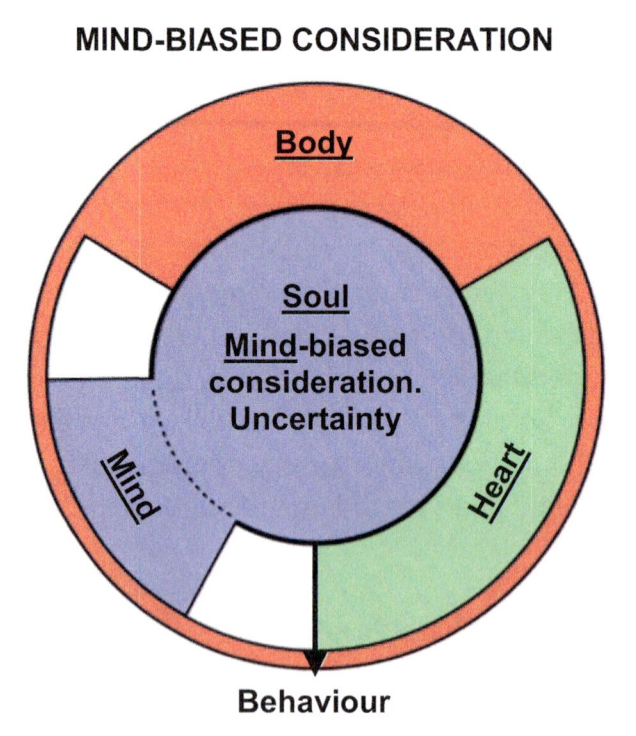

MIND-BIASED CONSIDERATION

Body

Soul
Mind-biased consideration.
Uncertainty

Mind

Heart

Behaviour

HEART-BIASED CONSIDERATION

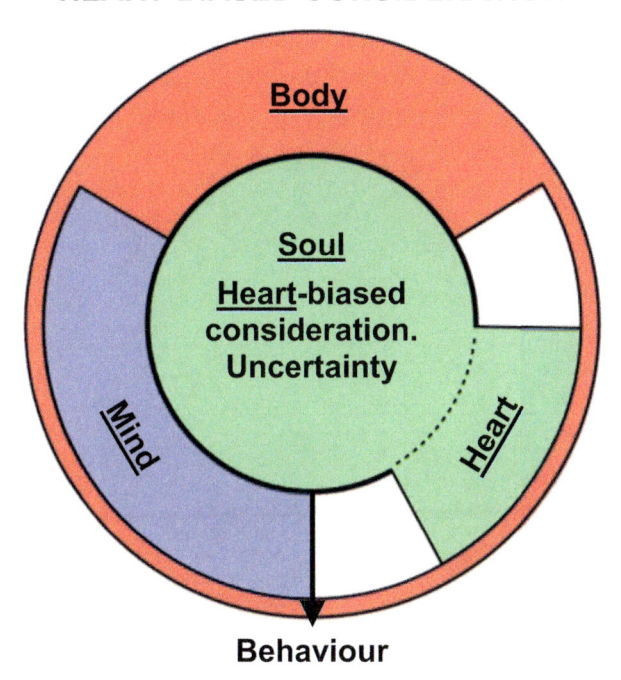

Body

Soul
Heart-biased consideration.
Uncertainty

Mind

Heart

Behaviour

BODY-BIASED CONSIDERATION

Body

Soul
Body-biased consideration.
Uncertainty

Mind

Heart

Behaviour

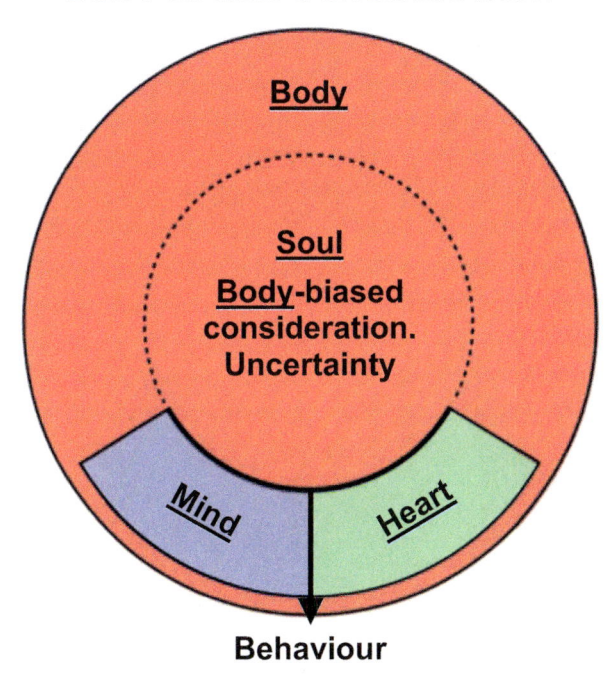

Chapter 16

THE SIX
BIAS EFFECTS

Since there are three biased person types and two degrees of bias, there are six bias effects. The six bias effects are:

The distinct mind obsession
The extreme mind obsession
The distinct heart obsession
The extreme heart obsession
The distinct body addiction
The extreme body addiction

The Distinct Mind Obsession

A person who has a distinct mind-biased consideration will have a distinct mind obsession. This means that they will have a distinct obsession with having truthful opinions and the associated chemical serotonin in their mind, and little interest in having gracious cares in their heart or righteous feelings in their body. So, this person will be distinctly compulsive, suspicious and detached.

The Extreme Mind Obsession

A person who has an extreme mind-biased consideration will have an extreme mind obsession. This means that they will have an extreme obsession with having truthful opinions and the associated chemical serotonin in their mind, and no interest in having gracious cares in their heart or righteous feelings in their body. So, this person will be extremely compulsive, suspicious and detached, which mainstream psychology terms "OCD, Paranoid and Schizoid", respectively.

The Distinct Heart Obsession

A person who has a distinct heart-biased consideration will have a distinct heart obsession. This means that they will have a distinct obsession with having gracious cares and the associated chemical oxytocin in their heart, and little interest in having righteous feelings in their body or truthful opinions in their mind. So, this person will be distinctly sensitive, emotional and needy.

The Extreme Heart Obsession

A person who has an extreme heart-biased consideration will have an extreme heart obsession. This means that they will have an extreme obsession with having gracious cares and the associated chemical oxytocin in their heart, and no interest in having righteous feelings in their body or truthful opinions in their mind. So, this person will be extremely sensitive, emotional and needy, which mainstream psychology terms "Avoidant, Bipolar and Dependent", respectively.

The Distinct Body Addiction

A person who has a distinct body-biased consideration will have a distinct body addiction. This means that they will have a distinct addiction to having unrighteous feelings and the associated chemical dopamine in their body, and little interest in having truthful opinions in their mind or gracious cares in their heart. So, this person will be distinctly dramatic, delusional and grandiose.

The Extreme Body Addiction

A person who has an extreme body-biased consideration will have an extreme body addiction. This means that they will have an extreme addiction to having unrighteous feelings and the associated chemical dopamine in their body, and no interest in having truthful opinions in their mind or gracious cares in their heart. So, this person will be extremely dramatic, delusional and grandiose, which mainstream psychology terms "Histrionic, Narcissistic and Antisocial", respectively.

DISTINCT MIND OBSESSION

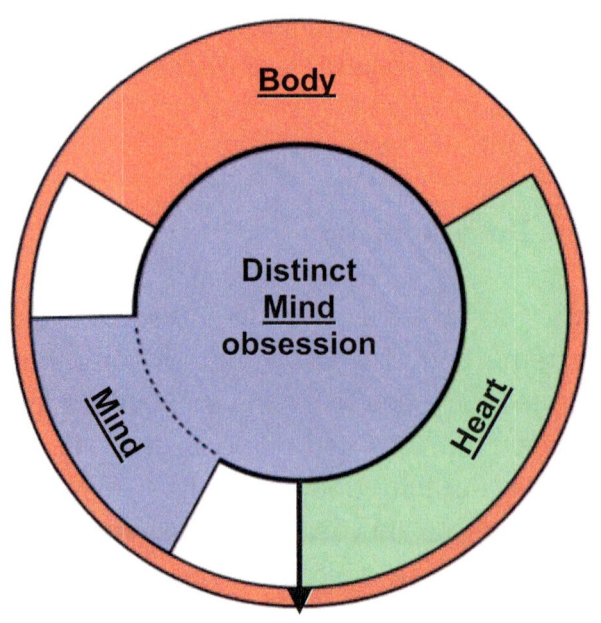

Compulsive, suspicious & detached

EXTREME MIND OBSESSION

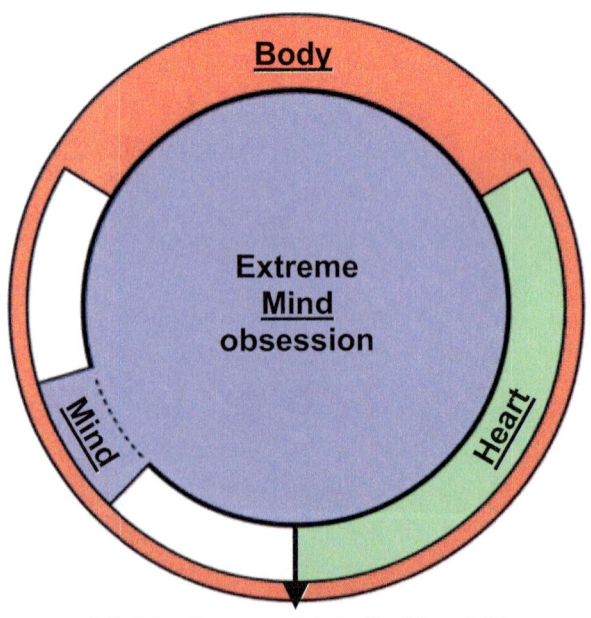

"OCD, Paranoid & Schizoid"

DISTINCT HEART OBSESSION

Body

Distinct **Heart** obsession

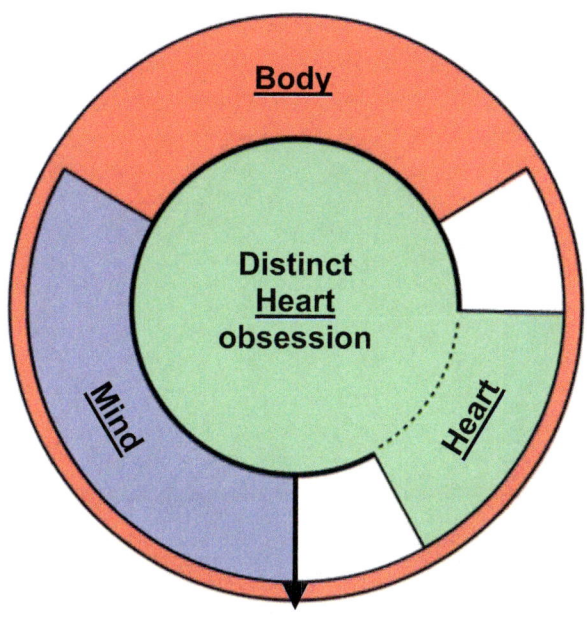

Mind

Heart

Sensitive, emotional & needy

EXTREME HEART OBSESSION

Body

Extreme **Heart** obsession

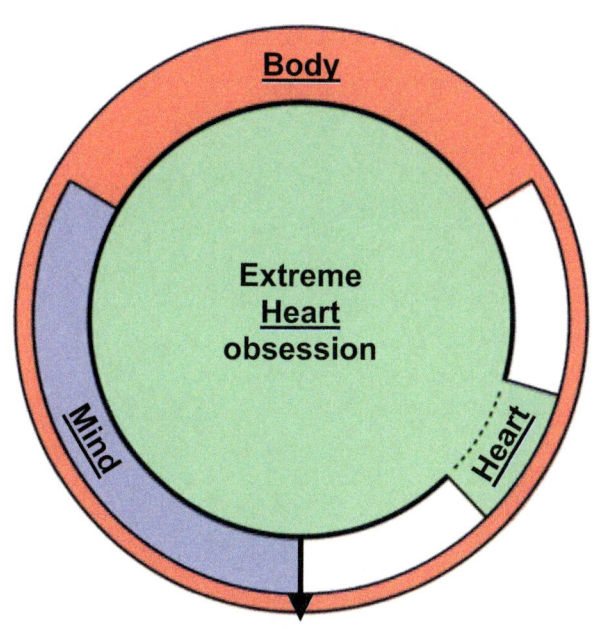

Mind

Heart

"Avoidant, Bipolar & Dependent"

DISTINCT BODY ADDICTION

Body

Distinct **Body** addiction

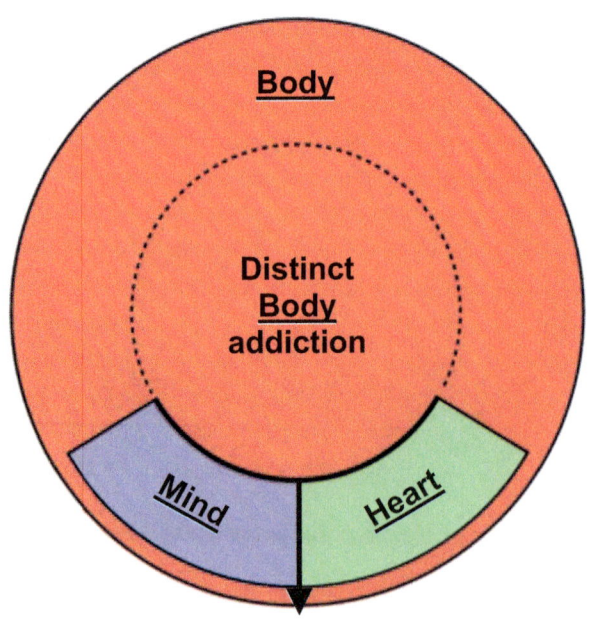

Mind | **Heart**

Dramatic, delusional & grandiose

EXTREME BODY ADDICTION

Body

Extreme **Body** addiction

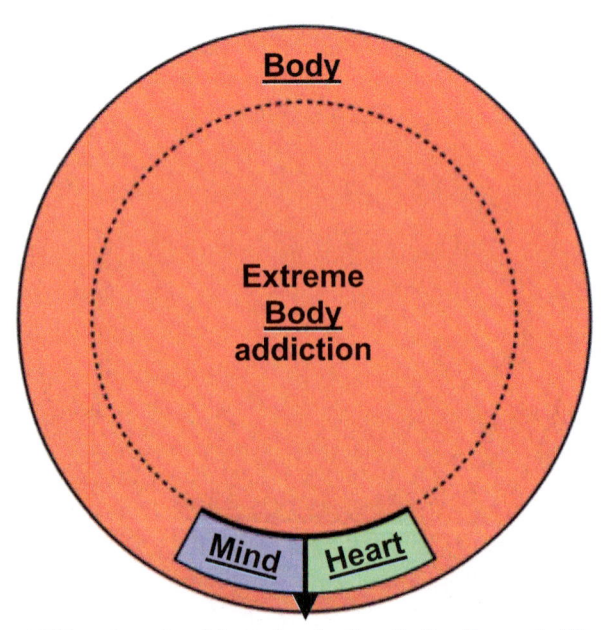

Mind | **Heart**

"Histrionic, Narcissistic & Antisocial"

Chapter 17

THE THREE BIAS SOLUTIONS

Since there are three bias problems, there are three bias solutions. The three bias solutions are:

The mind-biased consideration solution
The heart-biased consideration solution
The body-biased consideration solution

The Mind-Biased Consideration Solution

A mind-biased person needs a solution to their mind-biased consideration. This means that they need a solution to their over consideration of the insufficient truthful knowledge in their mind, and to their inconsideration of any gracious understanding in their heart or righteous experience in their body. So, this person needs gracious understanding to form gracious cares in their heart, righteous experience to form righteous feelings in their body, and then an increase of truthful knowledge to increase the truthful opinions in their mind.

The Heart-Biased Consideration Solution

A heart-biased person needs a solution to their heart-biased consideration. This means that they need a solution to their over consideration of the insufficient gracious understanding in their heart, and to their inconsideration of any righteous experience in their body or truthful knowledge in their mind.

So, this person needs righteous experience to form righteous feelings in their body, truthful knowledge to form truthful opinions in their mind, and then an increase of gracious understanding to increase the gracious cares in their heart.

The Body-Biased Consideration Solution

A body-biased person needs a solution to their body-biased consideration. This means that they need a solution to their over consideration of the excess unrighteous experience in their body, and to their inconsideration of any truthful knowledge in their mind or gracious understanding in their heart. So, this person needs truthful knowledge to form truthful opinions in their mind, gracious understanding to form gracious cares in their heart, and then an increase of righteous experience to increase the righteous feelings in their body.

MIND-BIASED CONSIDERATION SOLUTION

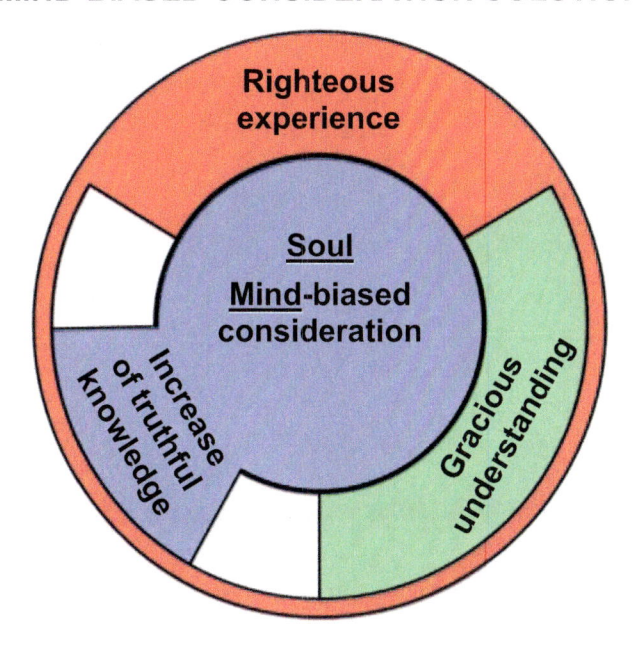

- Righteous experience
- Soul: **Mind**-biased consideration
- Increase of truthful knowledge
- Gracious understanding

HEART-BIASED CONSIDERATION SOLUTION

- Righteous experience
- Soul: **Heart**-biased consideration
- Truthful knowledge
- Increase of gracious understanding

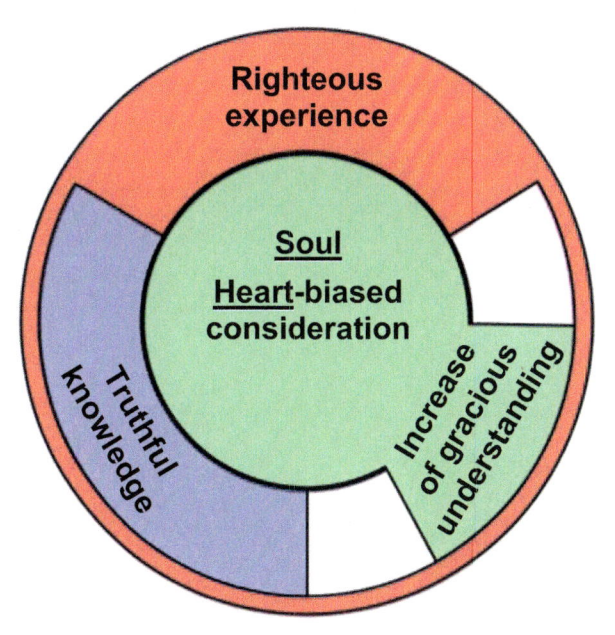

BODY-BIASED CONSIDERATION SOLUTION

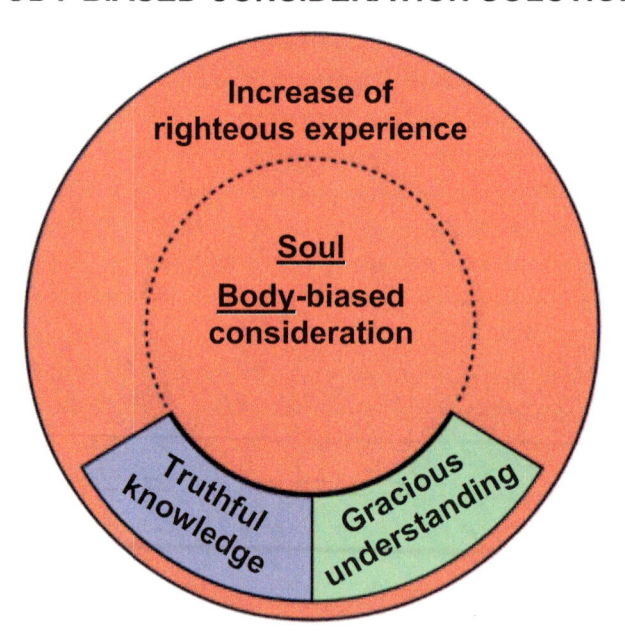

- Increase of righteous experience
- **Soul**
- **Body**-biased consideration
- Truthful knowledge
- Gracious understanding

Chapter 18

THE THREE BIAS TREATMENTS

Since there are three biased person types, there are three bias treatments. Prov 3:11 & 8:33 & 15:31; 2 Tim 3:16; Rom 3:16 [KJV]. The three bias treatments are:

The mind-biased person treatment
The heart-biased person treatment
The body-biased person treatment

The Mind-Biased Person Treatment

A mind-biased person needs the appropriate treatment for their mind-biased consideration. This means that they need treatment for their over consideration of the insufficient truthful knowledge in their mind, and for their inconsideration of any gracious understanding in their heart or righteous experience in their body. So, firstly this person needs to have relevant gracious understanding instructed into them by it being explained to them, in order for this gracious understanding to form gracious cares in their heart. Secondly, in conjunction with gracious understanding, they need to have relevant righteous experience induced in them by it being described to them, in order for this righteous experience to form righteous feelings in their body. Thirdly, after they illustrate gracious cares and righteous feelings, they will need to have the untruthful knowledge in them corrected with an increase of relevant truthful knowledge by it being told to them, in order for this truthful knowledge to increase the truthful opinions in their mind. Then this person will have the competence to be just, kind, and right, towards some people.

The Heart-Biased Person Treatment

A heart-biased person needs the appropriate treatment for their heart-biased consideration. This means that they need treatment for their over consideration of the insufficient gracious understanding in their heart, and for their inconsideration of any righteous experience in their body or truthful knowledge in their mind. So, firstly this person needs to have relevant righteous experience induced in them by it being described to them, in order for this righteous experience to form righteous feelings in their body. Secondly, in conjunction with righteous experience, they need to have relevant truthful knowledge infused into them by it being told to them, in order for this truthful knowledge to form truthful opinions in their mind. Thirdly, after they illustrate righteous feelings and truthful opinions, they will need to have an increase of relevant gracious understanding instructed into them by it being explained to them, in order for this gracious understanding to increase the gracious cares in their heart. Then this person will have the competence to be just, kind, and right, towards some people.

The Body-Biased Person Treatment

A body-biased person needs the appropriate treatment for their body-biased consideration. This means that they need treatment for their over consideration of the excess unrighteous experience in their body, and for their inconsideration of any truthful knowledge in their mind or gracious understanding in their heart. So, firstly this person needs to have relevant truthful knowledge infused into them by it being told to them, in order for this truthful knowledge to form truthful opinions in their mind. Secondly, in conjunction with truthful knowledge, they need to have relevant gracious understanding instructed into them by it being explained to them, in order for this gracious understanding to form gracious cares in their heart. Thirdly, after they illustrate truthful opinions and gracious cares, they will need to have the unrighteous experience in them reproved with an increase of relevant righteous experience by it being described to them, in order for this righteous experience to increase the righteous feelings in their body. Then this person will have the competence to be just, kind, and right, towards some people.

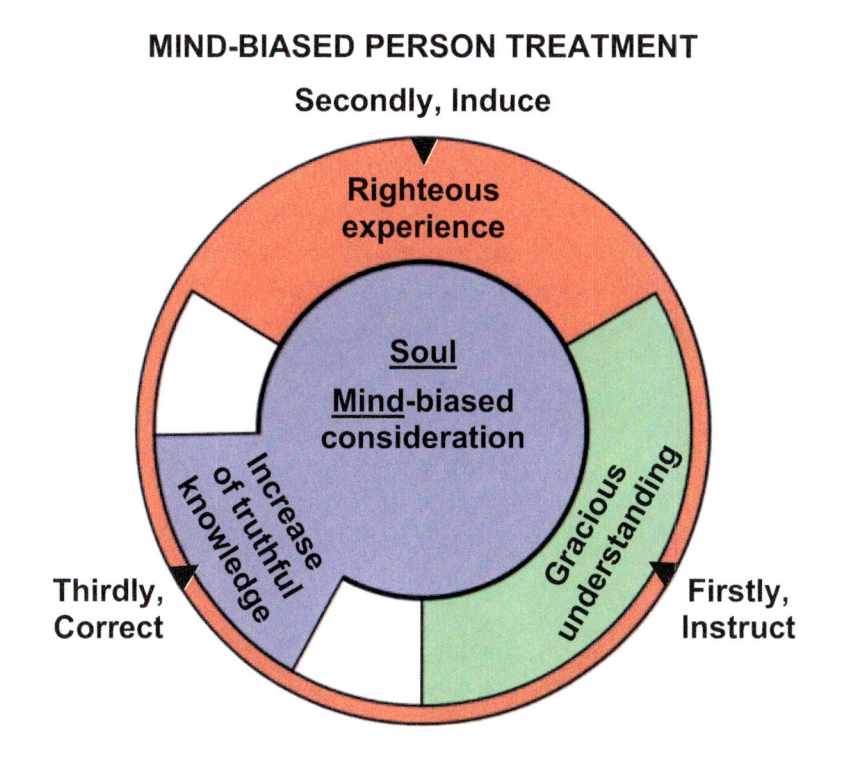

MIND-BIASED PERSON TREATMENT

Secondly, Induce

Righteous experience

Soul
Mind-biased consideration

Increase of truthful knowledge

Gracious understanding

Thirdly, Correct

Firstly, Instruct

HEART-BIASED PERSON TREATMENT

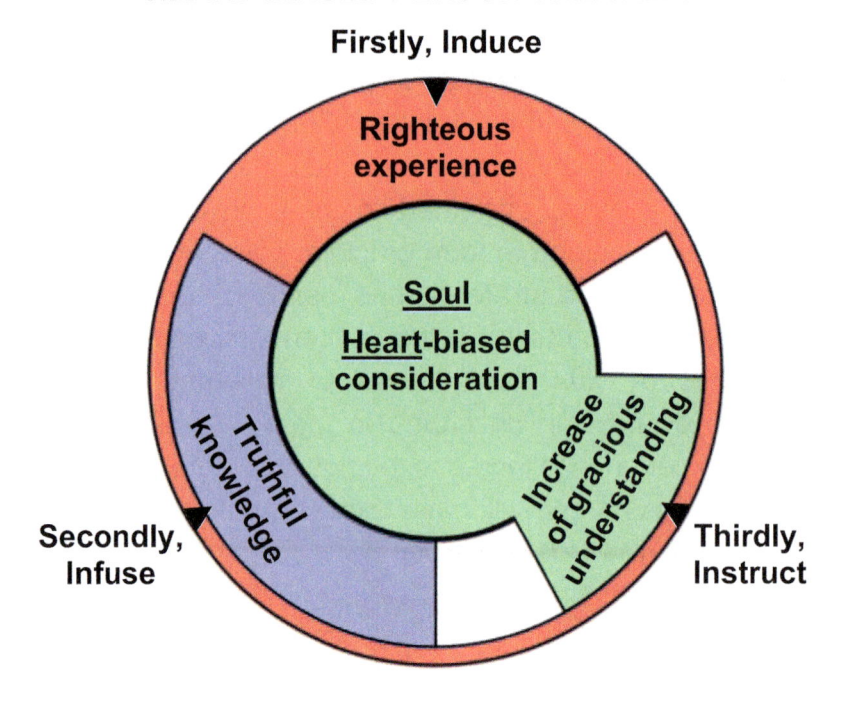

Firstly, Induce

Righteous experience

Soul
Heart-biased consideration

Truthful knowledge

Increase of gracious understanding

Secondly, Infuse

Thirdly, Instruct

BODY-BIASED PERSON TREATMENT

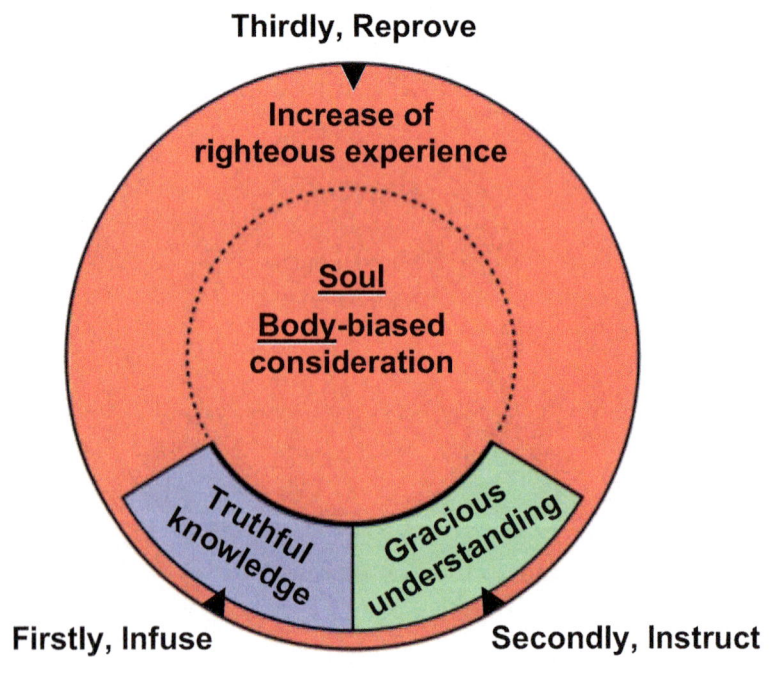

Thirdly, Reprove

Increase of righteous experience

Soul
Body-biased consideration

Truthful knowledge

Gracious understanding

Firstly, Infuse

Secondly, Instruct

Chapter 19

THE FOUR SPIRITUAL DEVELOPMENT STAGES

Just as there are four physical development stages to physical birth, namely, acceptance, fertilization, implantation and gestation, there are four spiritual development stages to spiritual birth. Matt 5:3-6 [KJV]. The four spiritual development stages are:

The accepting stage
The grieving stage
The submitting stage
The filling stage

The Accepting stage

Stage one of spiritual development is a person feeling poor in spirit due to experiencing the righteousness of Christ, God's Word. Jn 1:1-3 & 14 [KJV]. This means that they accept the righteous feeling in their body that they lack the competence to be just, kind, and right, towards all people, having been peacefully persuaded to accept their divine purpose by truth from the Bible.

This first stage of spiritual development corresponds to the first stage of physical development in the womb, which is the egg accepting that it lacks the competence to fulfil its purpose, having been persuaded to accept its purpose by the sperm.

The Grieving Stage

Stage two of spiritual development is a person mourning due to understanding the kindness of Christ, God's Word. This means that they grieve in their heart, having had Christ's gracious cares formed in them by gracious understanding from the Bible.

This second stage of spiritual development corresponds to the second stage of physical development in the womb, which is the egg suffering, having had a new nature formed in it by the sperm.

The Submitting Stage

Stage three of spiritual development is a person meekly submitting to the justness of Christ, God's Word. This means that they humbly submit their mind to having Christ's truthful opinions formed in them by truthful knowledge from the Bible.

This third stage of spiritual development corresponds to the third stage of physical development in the womb, which is the egg submitting itself to having essential systems formed in it by essential nutrients from the uterus.

The Filling Stage

Stage four of spiritual development is a person hungering and thirsting for more righteousness from Christ, God's Word. This means that they hungrily fill their mind with Christ's truthful knowledge and thirstily fill their heart with Christ's gracious understanding regarding God's will from the Bible.

This fourth stage of spiritual development corresponds to the fourth stage of physical development in the womb, which is when the baby must be fully nourished in order to properly develop.

FOUR SPIRITUAL DEVELOPMENT STAGES

Stage 4 **Filling**	Fill mind with Christ's truthful knowledge & heart with Christ's gracious understanding
Stage 3 **Submitting**	Submit mind to Christ's truthful opinions
Stage 2 **Grieving**	Grieve in heart due to Christ's gracious cares
Stage 1 **Accepting**	Accept in body the righteous feeling of incompetence

Matt 5:3-6 [KJV].

Chapter 20

THE THREE CHRIST-ATTESTATION LEVELS

Just as there are three levels of self-attestation, namely, telling in babyhood, demonstrating and explaining in childhood, and persuading in puberty, there are three levels of Christ-attestation. Matt 5:7-9; 13:23 [KJV]. The three levels of Christ-attestation are:

Attestation to Christ's justness
Attestation to Christ's kindness
Attestation to Christ's rightness

Attestation to Christ's Justness

Level one of Christ-attestation is a spiritually born person attesting to the justness of Christ. This means that they practice being just, towards all people, like Christ, and mercifully telling merely physically born people their truthful knowledge from the Bible of Christ's justness. 2 Cor 2:14 [KJV].

This first level of Christ-attestation corresponds to the first level of self-attestation, which is a person in babyhood telling what they know to other people.

Attestation to Christ's Kindness

Level two of Christ-attestation is a spiritually born person attesting to the kindness of Christ. This means that they practice being kind, towards all people, like Christ, and unpretentiously demonstrating and explaining to merely physically born people their gracious understanding from the Bible of Christ's kindness. Phili 2:15 [KJV].

This second level of Christ-attestation corresponds to the second level of self-attestation, which is a person in childhood demonstrating and explaining what they understand to other people.

Attestation to Christ's Rightness

Level three of Christ-attestation is a maturing spiritually born person attesting to the rightness of Christ. This means that they practice being right, towards all people, like Christ, and peacefully persuading merely physically born people to accept their own divine purpose of attesting to the justness, kindness and rightness of Christ. Acts 26:28-29 [KJV].

This third level of Christ-attestation corresponds to the third level of self-attestation, which is a maturing person in puberty persuading other people to be like them.

Every person who is persuaded to accept their divine purpose, will accept the righteous feeling in their body that they lack the competence to be just, kind, and right, towards all people, like Christ. Lk 6:31-35; Jn 15:12 [KJV]. This means that they accept that they lack the truthful knowledge, gracious understanding and righteous experience, from the Bible, which they need in order to have the competence to attest to the justness, kindness and rightness of Christ. So, this person will then complete the four spiritual development stages, and progress through the three Christ-attestation levels [Chapters 19 & 20].

THREE CHRIST- ATTESTATION LEVELS

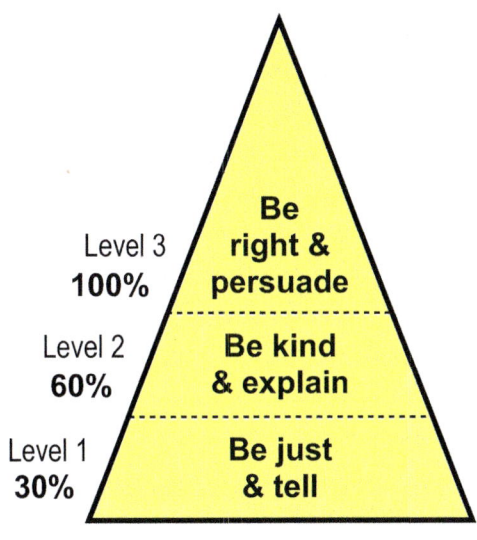

Level 3 **100%** — **Be right & persuade**
Level 2 **60%** — **Be kind & explain**
Level 1 **30%** — **Be just & tell**

Matt 5:7-9; 13:23 [KJV].

Chapter 21

THE TWO MEANINGS OF LIFE

Since there are two views of psychology, namely, mainstream and biblical, there are two definitions of the meanings of life. The two definitions of the meanings of life are:

The realization of full potential
The fulfilment of divine purpose

The Realization of Full Potential

According to mainstream psychology, the meaning of life is for a person to realize their full potential, which is to progress through levels of self-actualization - actualization of one's true self and full capabilities.

For a person to realize their full potential, they must first complete four stages of personal growth by following their heart and gratifying their ego. And the ultimate reward for realizing their full potential is mental transcendence from a limited to a higher consciousnesss.

Mainstream psychology's four stages of personal growth are:

Material gain - food, water, shelter and rest.
Safety gain - health, money and security.
Social gain - family, friends and sexual intimacy.
Esteem gain - achievements, success and respect.

Mainstream psychology's self-actualization includes:

Actualization of moral best.
Actualization of intellectual best.
Actualization of creative best.

Mainstream psychology uses a pyramid [the Maslow's Hierarchy of Needs] to illustrate a person's ascension through their four stages of personal growth to self-actualization and transcendence, because they are stages of self-improvement.

The Fulfilment of Divine Purpose

According to biblical psychology, the meaning of life is for a person to fulfil their divine purpose, which is to progress through the three levels of Christ-attestation - attestation to the justness, kindness and rightness of Christ, God's Word. 1 Cor 6:20; 10:31; Jn 1:1 & 14 [KJV].

For a person to fulfil their divine purpose, they must first complete the four stages of spiritual development by doing what Christ says in the Bible and subduing their body-lusts. Matt 7:24-27; 1 Cor 9:27 [KJV]. And the ultimate reward for fulfilling their divine purpose is literal transference from Earth to God's presence. 1 Thess 4:17 [KJV].

Biblical psychology's four stages of spiritual development are:

Curb esteem - by accepting righteous feeling of incompetence.
Curb social - by grieving due to Christ's gracious cares.
Curb safety - by submitting to Christ's truthful opinions.
Curb material - by filling with Christ's truthful knowledge and Christ's gracious understanding.

Biblical psychology's three levels of Christ-attestation are:

Attest to Christ's justness - by being just towards all people, like Christ, and telling knowledge of Christ's justness.

Attest to Christ's kindness - by being kind towards all people, like Christ, and demonstrating and explaining understanding of Christ's kindness.

Attest to Christ's rightness - by being right towards all people, like Christ, and persuading experience of Christ's rightness.

Biblical psychology flips the first four layers of mainstream psychology's pyramid, to illustrate a person's ascension through the four stages of spiritual development to Christ-attestation and transference, because they are stages of self-denial. So, these four stages are the complete opposite and reverse of mainstream psychology's four stages of ascension through personal growth to self-actualization and transcendence.

THE REALIZATION OF FULL POTENTIAL

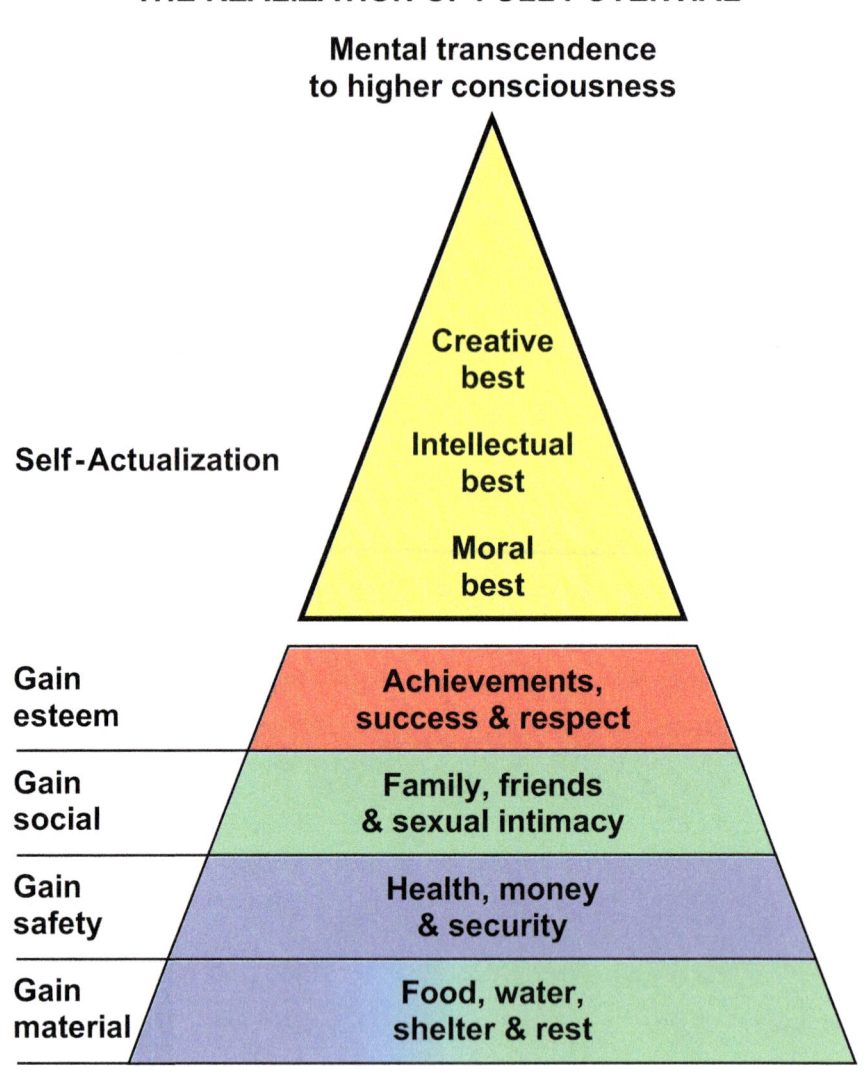

Mental transcendence to higher consciousness

Self-Actualization
- Creative best
- Intellectual best
- Moral best

Gain esteem — Achievements, success & respect

Gain social — Family, friends & sexual intimacy

Gain safety — Health, money & security

Gain material — Food, water, shelter & rest

Self-Improvement

Mainstream psychology says that a person must seek personal gain through self-improvement, in order to be content with their life by being their best.

THE FULFILMENT OF DIVINE PURPOSE

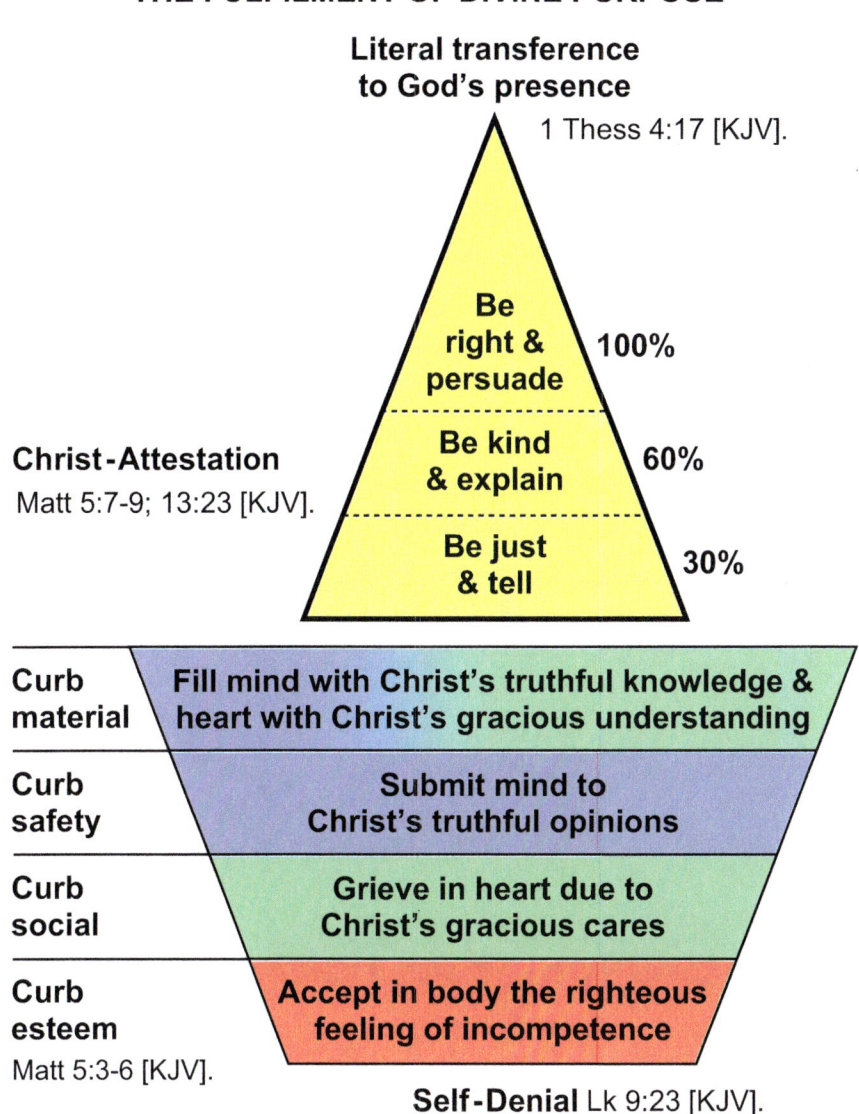

Literal transference to God's presence
1 Thess 4:17 [KJV].

Christ-Attestation
Matt 5:7-9; 13:23 [KJV].

- Be right & persuade — 100%
- Be kind & explain — 60%
- Be just & tell — 30%

Curb material	Fill mind with Christ's truthful knowledge & heart with Christ's gracious understanding
Curb safety	Submit mind to Christ's truthful opinions
Curb social	Grieve in heart due to Christ's gracious cares
Curb esteem	Accept in body the righteous feeling of incompetence

Matt 5:3-6 [KJV].

Self-Denial Lk 9:23 [KJV].

Biblical psychology says that a person must seek spiritual gain through self-denial, in order to be content with their life by being like Christ.

Chapter 22

THE TWO TREATMENT AIMS

Since there are two views of psychology, namely, mainstream and biblical, there are two treatment aims. The two treatment aims are:

To aid in the realization of full potential
To aid in the fulfilment of divine purpose

To Aid in the Realization of Full Potential

Mainstream psychology is evolution theory based. This means that it is based upon the belief that people are evolved animals, that are instinctive and learn how to behave. So, the aim of mainstream psychology based treatment is to support, indulge and validate a person, in order to help them to learn to practice better behaviour.

The aim of mainstream psychology based treatment is to help a person to re-order their mind [or re-wire their brain] by self enlightenment, repetition and reward, so that they can realize their full potential.

Mainstream psychology based treatment is merely a crutch, because it focuses on a person's thoughts and behaviour - *the symptoms*, and de-emphasizes the reason for the thoughts and behaviour - *the cause*.

To Aid in the Fulfilment of Divine Purpose

Biblical psychology is creation belief based. This means that it is based upon the belief that people are created beings, that can consider and decide how to behave. So, the aim of biblical psychology based treatment is to reprove, correct and instruct a person, in order to convince them to decide to practice better behaviour.

The aim of biblical psychology based treatment is to help a person to consider all available relevant information through their body, mind and heart, so that they can fulfil their divine purpose.

Biblical psychology based treatment is actually a cure, because it focuses on the reason for a person's thoughts and behaviour - *the cause*, and emphasizes the person's ability to consider and decide how to behave - *the cure*.

Chapter 23

THE TWO PERSON MODELS

Since there are two views of psychology, namely, mainstream and biblical, there are two person models. The two person models are:

The Jung's person model
The Luke's person model

The Jung's Person Model

According to mainstream psychology, a person is only a mind. This means that a person has only one essential part, with a total of six working areas. So, a person's behaviour is determined by the six working areas of their one essential part. The six working areas are:

The persona
The ego
The shadow [inner child]
The soul image
The personality
The true self

The Luke's Person Model

According to biblical psychology, a person is a mind, a heart, a body, a soul, and a spirit. Mk 12:30; Heb 4:12 [KJV]. This means that a person has five essential parts, with a total of sixteen working areas. So, a person's behaviour is determined by the sixteen working areas of their five essential parts. The sixteen working areas are:

The knowledge area
The opinions area
The conceits area
The memories area
The understanding area
The cares area
The heart-lusts area
The emotions area
The experience area
The feelings area
The body-lusts area
The body-memory area
The conscience area
The consideration area
The decision area
The will area

There is no such thing as an ego, an id, or a superego.
There is no such thing as a shadow, or inner child.
There is no such thing as a soul image.
There is no such thing as a personality, or personality types.
There is no such thing as a true self.
There is no such thing as a subconsciousness.
There is no such thing as a preconsciousness.

THE JUNG'S PERSON MODEL

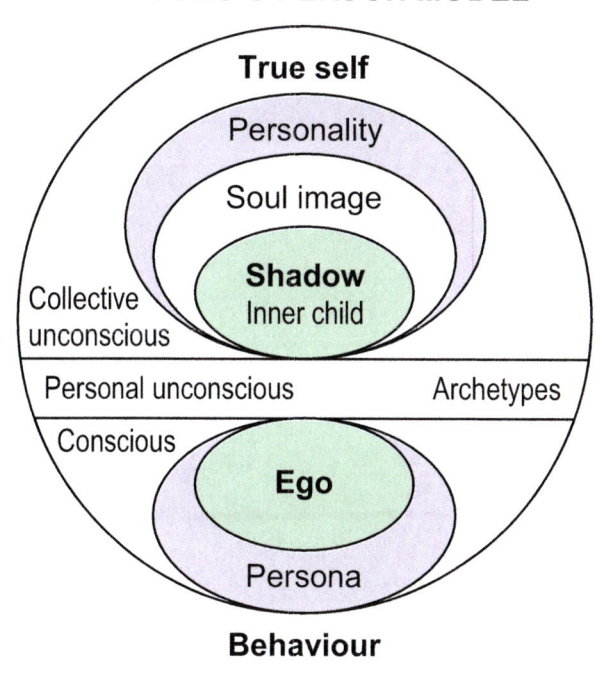

True self
- Personality
- Soul image
- **Shadow** / Inner child
- Collective unconscious
- Personal unconscious
- Archetypes
- Conscious
- **Ego**
- Persona

Behaviour

THE LUKE'S PERSON MODEL

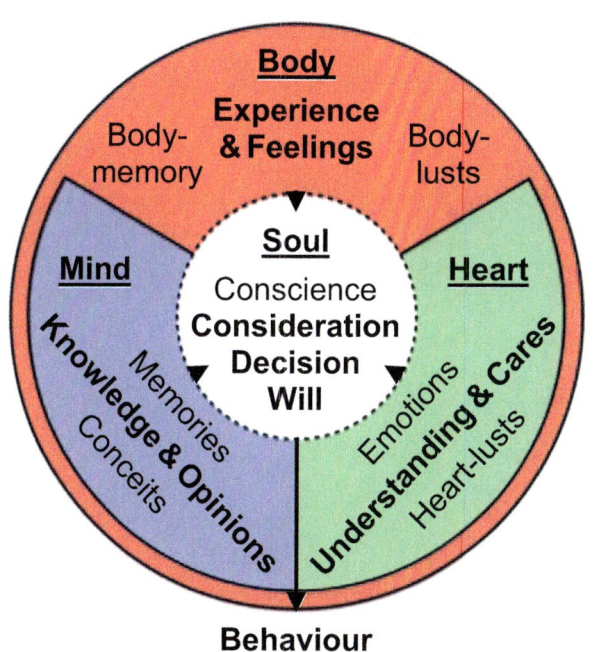

Body
- Experience & Feelings
- Body-memory
- Body-lusts

Soul
- Conscience
- **Consideration**
- **Decision**
- **Will**

Mind
- **Knowledge & Opinions**
- Memories
- Conceits

Heart
- **Understanding & Cares**
- Emotions
- Heart-lusts

Behaviour

Chapter 24

THE TWO DEFENSIVE MECHANISMS

Since there are two basic types of people, namely, biased and non-biased, there are two defensive mechanisms. The two defensive mechanisms are:

The deceitful defensive mechanism
The truthful defensive mechanism

The Deceitful Defensive Mechanism

According to mainstream psychology, an insecure person uses various defensive mechanisms [adaptive and maladaptive thoughts and behaviours] to defend themselves against threats to them realizing their full potential and being content with their life.

In actual fact, an insecure person uses only one defensive mechanism, and they use it ultimately to defend themselves against the righteous feeling of lack of competence in and of themselves.

This defensive mechanism is deceit, and it has sixteen main forms. The sixteen main forms are:

Avoidance - of feelings or thoughts by various means.
Isolation - of threatening feelings by incomplete consideration.
Dissociation - of self from reality by tiredness or stupidity.
Undoing - of feelings by rumination over previous events.

Conversion - of psychological problems into physiological ones.
Denial - of knowledge to avoid facing consequences.
Repression - of knowledge so that it never enters consideration.
Suppression - of knowledge from entering consideration.
Humour - to mask anxiety, or to avoid a feeling or subject.
Compensation - for self dissatisfaction by self-improvement.
Sublimation - of unacceptable urges into a productive outlet.
Splitting - of things into extremes of either good or bad.
Regression - to an early developmental stage in their life.
Displacement - of their feelings towards another person.
Projection - of their threatening traits onto another person.
Introjection - of another person's opinions into their own.

The Truthful Defensive Mechanism

According to biblical psychology, every person should use only one defensive mechanism, and they should use it to defend themselves against threats to them fulfilling their divine purpose and being content with their life.

This defensive mechanism is truth, and it has seven main forms. Eph 6:11-18; 1 Pet 1:13; 1 Thess 5:8 [KJV]. The seven main forms are:

Loin girdle of truth - Christ's truthful opinions, in mind.
Breastplate of righteousness - Christ's gracious cares, in heart.
Boots of peace - willingness to be reconciled, in soul.
Shield of faith - faith in God's Word, in spirit.
Helmet of salvation - hope of salvation, in body.
Sword of Spirit - Christ's gracious understanding, in heart.
Word of God - Christ's truthful knowledge, in mind.

Printed in Great Britain
by Amazon